# UNAPOLOGETIC
## a generation that can't even

### TRACI PROPST

Published by: Traci Propst
Interior Design by: Voir Media Group

Cover Design by: voirmediagroup.com
Cover Photography: Voir Media Studio
Editing by: Sara O'Connor


ISBN: 978-0-692-10881-9
First Edition

# TABLE OF CONTENTS

# DEDICATION

I would like to dedicate this book to my fellow Millennial companions out there searching for all their own answers to life. May your journey be ever spontaneous, soulful, and fill you with gratitude because you're honestly amazing AF*.

"The biggest risk is not taking any risk. In a world that's changing really quickly, the only strategy that is guaranteed to fail is not taking risks."

-Mark Zuckerberg

# UNAPOLOGETIC DISCLAIMER

While I do have many valuable research sources cited, this book is mostly based on my personal experience and stories collected from peer groups. For those of you who are going to ask me to cite *every single* opinionated-statement I make, I won't be doing that. Sorry not sorry, this is not that type of book.

The truth is, it would be impossible for me to make these citations because the Millennial generation is in full-swing, and truthfully, we're not sure how this is all going to turn out in the end. We have already seen so many breakthroughs and mind-altering ideas within our generation, and those are what I'm going to discuss. I will be addressing both sides of topics. However, I am unapologetically on the Millennial's side of things – Duh.

I am also well aware that not *every single* Millennial reading this book will fit into *every single* one of these categories, because I don't either. It's not about whether you fit into them all or whether you agree or disagree, but more of an acceptance that this is how our generation is perceived as a whole.

This book is meant to be thought provoking, interesting, informative and an overall enjoyable read.

So, with that being said, just chill out, grab a glass of wine or whiskey, relax and read on.

# MILLENNIAL CODE

Anywhere you see an * in the book it means you can find the definition below. You're welcome.

- ❖ Adulting – behaving as a responsible adult regarding extremely mundane, but necessary tasks
- ❖ AF – As Fuck
- ❖ BRB – Be Right Back
- ❖ BS – Bull Shit
- ❖ Bye Felicia – you are dismissed, not in a good way.
- ❖ Catfished – to lure someone into an online relationship by pretending to be someone else
- ❖ CTFU- Cracking The Fuck Up
- ❖ Def – Definitely
- ❖ Hot Mess –unorganized and in total disarray
- ❖ IDGAF – I Don't Give A Fuck
- ❖ JK – Just Kidding
- ❖ LMAO – Laughing My Ass Off
- ❖ LOL – Laugh Out Loud
- ❖ NBD – No Big Deal

- ❖ OMG – Oh My God
- ❖ On the reg – on the regular
- ❖ OOTD – Outfit Of The Day
- ❖ Parentals – a parent unit of a child
- ❖ PC – Politically Correct
- ❖ POS – Parent Over Shoulder
- ❖ Prost – cheers in German
- ❖ Sips tea – the combination of honesty and gossip
- ❖ SMH – Shaking My Head (back and forth)
- ❖ Throwing shade – publicly criticizing someone
- ❖ TTYL – Talk To You Later
- ❖ Tweet – something we write and post on our Twitter account.
- ❖ WTF – What The Fuck

# FOREWORD

WE ARE THE MILLENNIALS. We are the first natively digital generation and have been both criticized and loved because of it. We are the promoters of the latest and biggest revolution: the Internet. We exemplify what it means to go everywhere (and get anything) with a click, yet are aware of how much responsibility goes along with it (though sometimes we don't exercise it well). We are using our digital upbringing to change the rules and chart a new course; however, Millennials are much more than simply innate, digitally oriented human beings.

Yes, sometimes we speak our own language and have our heads buried in our devices, but we also have two undisputable qualities: passion and loyalty. Our generation has to believe in something and, when we do, we go to the ends of the earth to support it.

Millennials are constantly being bombarded with information. We had to figure life out on our own when the economic models of our parents and grandparents became obsolete and ineffective. We have a voice, and I need all Millennials to read the following words very carefully: let us use this voice to support and uplift each other, now more than ever. We are capable of loving deeply; therefore let us learn from the past by demonstrating that we can humbly bring righteousness and goodness to those who will come after. Millennials care about our future leaders and creating a world that reflects our values.

Our generation must take risks on a daily basis (much differently than those who came before) and we have been unfairly chastised as unrealistic dreamers. History however shows us that real visionaries are those who change the status quo. We want to show you who we really are, without any pride or prejudice.

This book represents and exemplifies what the Millennial generation stands for: persistence, innovation, and above all else, happiness. When I met author Traci Propst, I wanted to support her work. We are both very like-minded when it comes to the desire of giving our generation a strong, solid voice. Both of us support this very positive movement and we will continue to uplift and motivate all of our neighboring leaders. Traci and I would like you to try to see it in this light, as an undertaking, more than simply as a generation.

Throughout this book, Traci discusses the obstacles we all face and shows us how to prevail over them. It also explains in detail the importance of understanding Millennials as a whole, and the enormous responsibility that our generation holds.

Seeing that many of us — including myself — are entrepreneurs, this book also serves as an encouraging guide on how to continue taking risks towards our goals and dreams. More so, it aids in continuing to push ourselves out of our comfort zones. We are all here on this planet to help each other and to make an impactful change for the generations to come.

Overall, this book is a feel-good read filled with thought-provoking concepts and imperative daily reminders. I am very excited for Traci's book, and I think you all will enjoy what she has to say regarding our unapologetic generation.

By purchasing this book, you are also supporting my charity - The Wishwall Foundation - and I want to thank all of you very much! As a Millennial, I am proud to be a dreamer who fights to make my wishes and those of others come true.

*-Simonetta Lein, The Wishmaker*
*Author, Named Top Influencer & Fashion Icon, Millennial Entrepreneur,*
*Activist Founder of The Wishwall Foundation*

# *the* **WISHWALL**
# **FOUNDATION**

The WISHWALL is a symbol of peace, hope, and unity in your community. Created by The Wishwall Foundation- a non-profit charitable organization founded by Simonetta Lein in 2015 and led by Raphael Amabile - that helps meaningful and socially impactful wishes come true via The Wishwall in every city and The Wishwall online, a worldwide online community. The Wishwall in every city is a physical wall where people gather for a two-day event and write down their wishes. It brings together community commitment, kindness, and peace. After the event, The Wishwall's Foundation Board of Directors selects one wish to grant, and The Wishwall will thereafter become a permanent mural and artistic attraction in the host city. Contact us to host The Wishwall in your city, help grant a wish, volunteer, or donate via PayPal at info@thewishwallfoundation.org

## #BUILDTHEWISHWALL

Visit The Wishwall at http://www.thewishwall.org

# PREFACE

Over a six-month period, in the beginning stages of writing this book, I noticed the number 911 everywhere — on a clock, a street sign, bills; no matter where I looked, there it was, staring me in the face. As much as I tried to blame it on coincidence, I became paranoid. Considering the obvious fact that it's an American distress call and the date of one of our country's biggest tragedies, I didn't accept it as a positive omen.

Equally bizarre was this; I woke up one morning, one week before my scheduled trip to Paris for a two-week vacation with my, then boyfriend, and immediately looked at the clock; 9:11. *WTF*\*! I spiraled into a full-blown panic attack and concluded: *this was definitely a sign*! Yup, I'm going to die. Who should I warn? Should I cancel my trip? I felt as though someone was sending me a signal over and over that I shouldn't be ignoring.

My anxiety hit a coasting high.

I decided to look up the meaning of this number (other than those that were already haunting me) with a Millennial-typical quick web search. I typed in SEEING THE NUMBER 911 EVERYWHERE. I was sure that I would find an article promising my untimely demise, but to my surprise, the results I found were not at all what I had expected…

"Angel numbers" reappeared as I skimmed through several websites. *Pleasantly* shocked, I read that the number "9" resonates with the attributes of the Universal Spiritual Laws, which are compassion, benevolence, and generosity: living life as a positive example, leadership, service to humanity, and light.

The number "11" is a Karmic Master Number which presents attributes of illumination, enlightenment, inspiration, alternate consciousness, mysticism, sensitivity, enthusiasm, and creativity[1,2].

As it turns out, the number 911 wasn't a bad omen at all, but an extremely powerful vibration! According to the articles, the combination indicated that "the angels" were trying to tell me that a new door had opened as a product of my positive thoughts, intentions, and actions. It's a sign to make the most of an opportunity and walk forward with confidence and assurance that I am fulfilling part of my "karmic destiny"[1,2].

Considering all the doubt and fear I had in writing this book and my ability to reach others through it, I accepted my "Angel Numbers", put all fear aside, and went forward full force. In fact, I now *embrace* seeing 911 and end up with a dumb smirk on my face.

The core of this preface, other than self-reassurance, resonates with the theme throughout the book; perspective creates ideas and situations.

Everything is not always how it seems, in fact, it

rarely is. Just by altering your perspective, it will change your entire perception of the things around you and can lead to having a much more positive mindset and life overall.

Keeping that in mind, I hope you accept my efforts to break down and elaborate on our incredible Millennial generation. I am very proud to present this book including all the aforementioned celestial positivity of the 911 number and more.

Millennials are the dopest generation and here is why.

# *INTRO*
# THE SHIT YOU DON'T CARE ABOUT

I'm going to share a little background about myself and why I decided to write this book. I am the epitome of what a first world Millennial looks like. I am a success-driven, anxious, optimistic, socially innovative, risk-taker. I am a college-educated woman who still tends to make choices with my desires instead of my brain. I believe in a universal God, the Law of Attraction, and that happiness is a choice. I try to focus on competing with no one other than myself. Competing with and comparing yourself to others is a complete waste of time. Instead, I learn from them.

In retrospect, everything I have been through -- all the places I have lived, all the people I met while growing up, and all the experiences I have had – have made me into exactly who I am today, and I appreciate the tough skin, yet free nature, it instilled within me.

I'm sharing this because I feel that in order for you

to fully understand my voice and my thought process, it's important you first understand where I come from. While some of the stories in this book are personal and uncomfortable, I'm sharing them anyway so you can see the full picture.

I grew up a military brat, attending numerous schools, and living in many different states and one other country before my dad retired as a Lieutenant Colonel from the U.S. Army. This is a lifestyle not many children grow up accustomed to. For me, it was extremely difficult always being the new kid in school and trying to navigate who I really was and where I belonged. My experiences varied from place to place, and my perspective on life changed from town to town.

However, a positive that came out of this is I have a chameleon's personality (in a non-fake way) and thus I find myself relatable to most people I meet. I have experienced both extremes growing up: sometimes I was the popular girl, and other times I was bullied. I met some of the most kind-hearted and cruelest peers throughout my travels, because let's face it; kids can be fucking MEAN. Some of them had a significant impact on me, and in many instances unknowingly changed my life and how I, to this day, view the world. Either way, it created a very strong voice and opinion within me.

Alongside being brought up in a moving military family, I was raised a Christian, having to uphold not only the semi-strict military expectations, but also religious values. I was brought up in a household where we attended church regularly, chores were expected, a small allowance was given, my tongue felt the punishment of hot sauce when I was disrespectful, and spankings were shelled out on the reg* when my sister and I acted out.

I was always a very outspoken and expressive child who considered herself to be a free spirit—a free spirit who was constantly testing the waters. Always determined to experience a journey worth writing about. Since I can remember, casual writing has always been a part of my life, having kept a diary since age seven, documenting every stage of life.

However, at this point in my life, I have come to the conclusion that it's not necessarily about having a jaw-dropping journey that matters, but what you take from your journey and, more importantly, how you apply it.

My adult journey started while attending Penn State University and obtaining a degree in Communication Arts & Sciences. Right after graduation I moved to Los Angeles to start my on-camera career, only to succumb to the harsh reality of being on my own at twenty-two, in my own skin, with not one familiar soul around. In less than a year, I retreated back to the familiarity of the East Coast and moved to New York City. I obtained a nine-to-five desk job which, aside from being in the television industry, had nothing to do with my on-camera hosting passion.

After two years of spending some time in the safety net of a nine to five and East Coast friends and family close by, I was able to recalibrate and decided what it was I wanted in life at the age of twenty-four. I decided that it was time to go back to LA, continue what I had started, and follow my dreams of becoming an on-camera television host. It was time to face my fears. I realized my passion was so much stronger than my self-doubt and if I didn't take the chance, it would be something that I would regret.

What I discovered is that I really just wanted a platform to get my message across, to somehow help others find their courage to do the same as I had done.

Throughout this road to discovery, there were some critical turning points in my life. A turning point can be best described as a moment where you react to a life-altering event; after which your life is never again quite the same. What I hope to do is share some of my turning points with you and how they have led me to be this version of myself, which I am still working on every single day.

I need to point out that ironically, most of the turning points were viewed by me as negative when they occurred (like moving to LA hopeful and then retreating back less than a year later. Pretty damn embarrassing.), yet they always turned out to be blessings in disguise. Aside from these blessings, I want to break down how being part of the Millennial generation enabled me to handle these situations differently and how beneficial it was.

So, to get to the point, what do I want you to take from this book?

As I share my personal stories (while ignoring vulnerability or being PC*), I want you to understand or even more so, try to relate. I want anyone who is feeling lost or unsure to be able to use this book as a tool to navigate through those feelings. This tool may either help you develop the courage to make life-changing decisions or aid you in realizing that it is okay, and dare I say "normal" to feel unsure about some things, or even EVERYthing for that matter. Understand that your opinions, beliefs, jobs, friends, financial struggles, and living situation may constantly fluctuate—and that's okay! Embrace the change.

Look at each day as a new experience and a chance to learn. You should expect to be an extremely different person at the age of twenty-one than you were at eighteen (duh). Even more so, you will be a very different person at the age of twenty-five and then again at thirty, and so forth. Enjoy these different stages and look back at each one with a tender, **understanding** attitude towards yourself for all that you've learned, the mistakes you've made, and how you have grown from them.

It is important to learn to accept yourself within this

decade, because (as many Millennial acknowledge) the time between your twenties into your thirties is a time to experiment and mold yourself into a person that you are capable of loving. So, go easy on yourself and give yourself a break every once in a while.

To those reading who are not part of the Millennial generation, I want to assure you too, that if you can grasp the concepts I put out there and open your mind to giving them a try, your life will be that much better. Not to mention you will now have a better understanding of our generation, which will give you the upper hand in business, marketing, and overall communication with us.

# AN *UNAPOLOGETIC*
# GENERATION

# ONE

There is a word to describe a generation that is never satisfied, has an attention span of five seconds, craves independence, follows their dreams, and eats what people call "rabbit food" (known as kale) for dinner: *Millennials.*

While the birth years that span the generation known as Generation Y (Millennials) are flexible, many researchers label them between the years of 1983 and 2000, making a millennial currently in 2018 anywhere from eighteen to thirty-five years old[3].

We have been labeled: trophy kids, natural entrepreneurs, spendthrifts, broke, socialists, narcissists, politically engaged, less religious, more spiritual, and one-hundred percent anxiety-driven. The list goes on and on.

We are a one-of-a-kind cohort. On Urban Dictionary's website, we are defined in part as "a special little snowflake" – lol how (obnoxiously) cute.

The Millennial Generation is very different from any preceding generation, but the jury is still out if this carefree, independent lifestyle will benefit us in the long run or if we will instead be known as the generation of lost children.

I am fascinated with my generation. If we're going to be defined by labels, let me go ahead and throw some out as well. We are passionate, driven, educated, social-innovators, tech-savvy, and we really do have a special brain wiring going on that sets us apart.

We were born with a fire in us, and it's all about finding what feeds that fire; and when we do, we're legit unstoppable.

*Un-fucking-stoppable.*

Once I figured out the power our generation held, the power that *I* held, the opportunities became endless, and my imagination transformed into life's blank canvas.

We've come to realize that life is what we make of it and IDGAF* if you like our sleeve tattoos, pink and blue hair, lumberjack beards, man buns, ripped jeans (yes, we bought them like that), and our entitled attitudes. It is what it is, and we are who we are.

That said, being "free" still seems to carry a lot of worldly responsibility, and our "IDGAF" lifestyle has left some of us right back where we originally started: at our parents' houses. Only this time, with a very expensive piece of paper in hand, a college degree. However, this seems to bother our parents more than us because after all, who doesn't like laundry service and free food? Just saying…

As Millennials, one of our main priorities is constantly working towards getting to know exactly who we are and transforming into the people we want to be.

With so many avenues and opportunities, why settle for anything less than our ideal? We play a daily scrimmage in our heads in hopes of *finding* ourselves, creating the best version of ourselves. So, the over-thinking begins. *Should I move? Change careers? Get married? Have kids? What would make me happy?* It can all be so exhausting.

One thing is for sure, we are no longer the generation of people who enjoy starting from the bottom of a company and working our way up, doing what others like to call "paying our dues". That takes way too much time, and considering most places weren't hiring when a large majority of our generation graduated (during one of the worst recessions since The Great Depression) we were forced to find another way.

Also, with people working later into life before their retirement, not as many positions are available, we just do not have the patience. Patience is a foreign word to us and one we're not interested in practicing. Waiting our turn in line just to take commands from another person? Hell no. That's not how we were wired. We were raised being told we were the best at absolutely everything and we were praised for all of our "hard" work and accomplishments, so if this isn't happening in present time, Bye-Felicia*.

We want the adventurous life, the exciting life, the rewarding life. We want to make the world a better place for ourselves and our peers. Millennials have been set up with the idea that anything is possible—so we simply do not take *no* for an answer. We turn people's criticism and doors-slammed-in-our-faces as fuel for our ambition. If there is a way, we will find it. If there isn't a way, then we will make one.

We use the most successful leaders and entrepreneurs of today as our inspiration, and so we ask ourselves—how did *they* do it?

Well, one thing that seems to prove true time and time again is that successful people analyze themselves every day. They think about what they hope to accomplish that day and in the future. Their past accomplishments and successes are just that – in the past. It's all about moving forward.

We Millennials see and learn from them and realize that if we want to be the best, we must constantly be growing and changing—never to become complacent and never to accept the word *no*. Does that philosophy bite us in the ass sometimes? Absolutely, but who cares? We're unapologetic and were going to keep pushing.

As complex as we sound, our generation is pretty basic. One similarity we have to previous generations is that we have two main categories in life that we consider when we think of success: money and happiness. Our goal? Obviously to combine the two. However, until we are able to do so, we will weigh the pros and cons as to what is worth pursuing to help us reach our goals. Once one of the categories seems too empty, we will move on to something else in order to fill that category, especially if that category is our happiness.

You might say, "Doesn't every generation want money and happiness?" Of course! But the part that really **differentiates us** from previous generations is that Millennials place way more value on our happiness than we do on our money. Don't get it twisted, this is not to say that we aren't money-hungry because we def* are, but unlike generations before us, we prioritize enjoying our daily life over working (to us "wasting") it away. So, if we're ultimately not happy, we'll be moving along shortly. It's that simple.

This is in our favor, considering we will not be stuck in those so called dead-end jobs; contributing very little of our innate talent and grinding through the daily motions in hopes of one day being happy after retiring in Hilton Head or Key West, like many in generations preceding us – no thanks. We want to live our best life now.

In order to accomplish this, becoming short-term unemployed is a risk we seem to be more than willing to take if it means regaining our happiness. I'm saying this having been technically unemployed or "freelance" as we in LA like to call it, for half of my adult life.

However, let me clarify. I have **never** been on unemployment.

I have always been able to live comfortably off of my savings from when I am working and without **ever** having to ask for help. So, with that being said, when I say being unemployed I don't mean mooching off the government or our parents! I mean depending on one's self and doing what it takes to survive and make it work until we find something that makes us happy again.

Our goal in life is to take chances, to follow our dreams rather than take zero risk and regret not doing so (see Mark Zuckerberg's quote in the beginning of the book).

That is who we are in a nutshell, an **unapologetic generation** that refuses to give up. Now, let me break down what exactly makes us so captivating.

# *IGNITING* **OUR PASSION**

# TWO

If there's one thing you should know, it's that Millennials were born with hearts of fire. Passion is engrained in our DNA. We thrive on searching for the next adventure and are rarely content for very long. We live in the moment, and in that moment, we feel present; we feel alive! Some other generations may say it's time for us to grow up, plan, and work towards our secure future, but we're in absolutely no rush.

A few years ago, when I was home for the holidays, I attended our annual high school get-together at one of the local bars. Since it has been over ten years since high school graduation, I actually enjoy seeing where everyone is at this point in our lives. What has changed, and has anything stayed the same?

I remember talking to a longtime friend of mine; he had played high school and college football and was definitely known to be a party boy. In college, he was "that kid", the one who was always drinking way too

31

much and getting sloppy, blackout drunk.

Since then, his football career had ended earlier than he would have liked and he told me he was currently living in Seattle, working at a job that he was less than thrilled about, but he was taking the time to figure out what it really was he wanted to do. He was working on launching an app for smartphones and ultimately wanted to be able to work from home. Shocking (lol).

Overall, he was happy with his life. He basically lived in a frat house; he had five male roommates who were his good friends, and they partied hard every weekend. He loved it!

Just out of curiosity, not expecting an answer with any substance, I asked him the dreaded questions, *"What's your plan? Are you ready to settle down?"* He paused and smiled.

"No, I'm not ready. I might start looking for a different job soon, but I love my life so why change it?"

I totally related to that response. While many would say this is irresponsible, I think he's right. Why is there an age when it is no longer acceptable in society to have roommates? Why can't we still party like frat boys on the weekend, even though college has ended, if our bills are being paid on time? Why do we need to "grow up" at a specific societal age?

Let's back up a few generations and think about why people had to grow up so quickly. If we think far enough back, it was for survival; people didn't live as long. They needed to have kids for manual labor, to help around the house and in the fields so they could harvest and survive.

Moving forward to our parents' generation, growing up fast to have a family was fairly common. The men immediately started working right out of college, sometimes even while in high school, in order to be the bread winners for the families they were making early on. The women either worked for extra income or stayed home to bear the children and tend to the housework—this was how most of them were raised, this was what they were taught life was all about. Being raised by your family until you can go off and have your own family and then watch your kids start THEIR own family and so forth. That was it. The end. To us Millennials – this feels very mundane.

For most Millennials I know, that's not the case anymore. Now, we have so many more options. After finishing school, and since some of us are taking our grand ole time picking out life partners and settling down, we aren't in such a hurry to become adults and take on all this responsibility, which ultimately results in what we perceive as more stress and less fun.

In reality, at this point in time, the only person we really need to take care of is ourselves, so as long as this is happening, we don't see enjoying ourselves as stunting our adult growth.

After speaking with that friend about growing up, I then ran into another friend at the same reunion. She now lives in Texas and works in a hair salon as a stylist, even though she received a college degree in finance. She talked about how she was dating and hadn't found the right person, but that work was pretty much her life, and she loved what she was doing—following her dream of owning her own salon someday, despite her unrelated degree that she felt forced to obtain.

She asked me if I had seen some of the photos online of a small portion of our friends that were having babies, bellowing out, "I can't even *imagine* that right now!" Her fire had been ignited in the hair industry, and she was living a life she loved, a family was the furthest thing from her current mind set. She was overly content and happy building her business.

My old acquaintances and I have gone in different directions, but we seem to have the same idea when it comes to being a "grown up." As I examine my personal life thus far, I think I am as grown up as I should be right now. I make a good living striving to do what I love. I live in a nice apartment, four blocks from the beach in Los Angeles. I drive a luxury brand new car. I take care of all my own personal finances, and I literally do whatever I want in order to live my life to the fullest. I don't think that "adult" society should ask any more from me or look down on my decisions because they don't fall within some set of expectations.

With so much to look forward to in the future, Millennials are okay with living their best life in the present, patiently waiting on what the future holds. Maybe finding the right life-partner, maybe having children, or maybe traveling solo to their hearts content.

Our focus now is to be healthy and happy as we work towards our passion. If we're meeting these basic needs, what's wrong with doing things a different way than generations have done before? Who's to say this is the wrong way?

As a headstrong and driven individual no one can tell me what I can and cannot do. The question in my head is never *is this possible?* But instead, *how am I going to make this happen?*

For me, writing has always been part of my life. It is the fire within me, the urge to share my awareness with the world and my encounters with our generation. It is worth investing the time because I have the passion to pass along the information that I know is bigger than me, and much more important.

For me, if this shared knowledge can encourage even *one* person to embrace their own passion or create a more positive mentality, then it will all be worth it— *that* is the igniting I'm referring to. The fire that drives us to do something, and instead of making excuses of why we can't, we just run with it.

We are all here to leave our mark in some way, and

although this book is only a very small mark for our generation, I know it is a stepping-stone in the right direction. To use our voice and experiences, both good and bad, and to guide others, is an immense privilege.

Millennials have a lot to gain from each other. As we continue to blaze the trail through our fierce pursuit of happiness, even if that means defying the norm, we will see it through. So, all the haters and naysayers can take a back seat and just watch.

Giving credit where credit is due, there have obviously been people in prior generations who found their passion and in doing so, sparked a flame, which has helped the Millennials tremendously. They helped us realize it was possible and we wanted to emulate their success.

The torch has been passed and it is now our responsibility to carry it through to future generations..." in the most positive way. Once you realize you have the ability to do this, the responsibility it carries will probably make you want to throw up, and then, it will just turn into a new way of life.

Figure out your passion, whatever ignites your fire, and blaze your own trail.

No one got anywhere in life feeling comfortable.

# DEFYING THE CORPORATE LADDER

# THREE

While we are the most educated generation in history by far (with over sixty-percent of adult Millennials having attended college at some point in their life)[4], most of us graduated during the recession and were thrown into real life unprepared. Recent findings reported that the overall unemployment rate for Millennials peaked at over 13 percent in 2010[4] (the year I graduated).

This left us tens of thousands of dollars in debt from school loans and with a *mandatory* education that couldn't even get us a job! We faced student loan debt at a record high—nearly quadrupling over the past decade. No one hiring, no one being promoted, and no one leaving their jobs to retire early either. We were left taking the limited jobs that were available, but for little or no pay. Originally, this left us with a very discouraged mindset – we felt like we had been set up for failure.

While our generation is the first to be expected to

have a bachelor's degree as a *minimum* qualification, it seemingly has such little value when it comes to actual degree-related job searches. We're left with nothing but an expensive piece of paper that we can matte and hang it on the wall - or put it in our parents' basement, where mine currently resides. It's a really messed up system.

When we reflect and think about this piece of paper that has not given us the career kick-start we expected, other than proving we graduated and can finish what we started, we have no choice but to question mandatory mainstream qualifications.

Honestly, why did we actually obtain a degree?

College was fun, and Millennials like myself, who attended well-known universities would say that college was one of the best times of their lives. However, is that what we're paying for, a good time? To be honest, I'm very proud of being a college graduate, but that is only because of society's affirmative reputation associated with it. We are brainwashed to think we're smarter because we were able to obtain a degree.

Penn State was a blast, and I was able to graduate with barely any debt, however, countless Millennials were not as lucky – not at all. Most graduate with tens of thousands of dollars in debt for information they may never use again.

To clarify, I'm not talking about doctors, lawyers, scientists, environmentalists; people with degrees where the education is actually much needed, but what about the rest of us? The business majors, marketing majors, communication majors? I probably could have YouTubed and researched my entire degree. Sorry not sorry – it's true.

When I look back on college I vividly remember the people, the parties, and Greek life. Everything social is what comes to mind. Sad to say, but I recall only a handful of courses where I absorbed what I felt was "useful" information that I continue to apply to my life, both work and personal. The other courses were placed in my mental file labeled BS* (not Bachelor of Sciences).

This is not to single out my university. After speaking with many peers from colleges all over, including Cornell, Ohio State, USC, UCLA, UNC, and even the University of London, this seems to be the casual norm. Needless to say, that is not what we intended to go to college for, to only remember a cluster of courses and mainstream social events. Did we pay for experiences and friends when we were supposed to be paying for a better education to teach us what we actually needed to know?

How has this become the norm?

While this case may not be the same for *all* of my readers, I know many people can relate to a certain extent.

In fact, a recent survey from CareerBuilder showed that forty-seven percent of college graduates did not find a first job that was related to their college major. That's nearly HALF of college grads that aren't using their degree upon graduation![6] It's all too common to meet a college graduate not applying their degree to their current job position, yet we are paying thousands to have the university's name put on our résumé showing that we "specialized" in an area. Why? Oh because it's "expected of us".

In addition, a Georgetown University study calculated a percentage of jobs that soon will, not just suggest, but *require* postsecondary education in 2018. They concluded twenty-three percent of employers will require **a minimum** of a bachelor's degree. This percentage has almost tripled from nine-percent in 1973—the decade when many of the baby boomers were graduating from college.[7]

If college is going to be considered mandatory and many of us will not be using our degree for its original purpose, the least that colleges can do is offer us multiple courses we can benefit from in the long run. Why don't some of the prerequisites include classes like: budgeting, professionalism in the workplace (including anti-sexual harassment training, which it seems we need so desperately these days), progressive communication with peers, interview procedures? Something seems wrong here.

While some institutes are slowly making this shift, many are lagging. Why aren't these *real-life* fundamentals being incorporated into our institutions immediately? Instead there are prerequisite classes we're all expected to take, no matter what major we're interested in, such as Econ 101, Bio 101, and Stat 200. Not saying these are *completely* worthless to all, but to majors like mine? Yes, they pretty much are.

The real-life courses I proposed above aren't even offered as electives at the majority of colleges and universities.

I remember my major required me to take at least two courses of biology. Being a part of the Liberal Arts department with a major in Communication, I thought this was the most ridiculous requirement ever. In turn, I put little effort or interest into these classes and ended up getting a C both semesters, and my GPA suffered. These needed to be replaced with more tech-savvy, humanistic, and arts-of-the-trade classes. True, we chose to go to a university and not a trade school; however, universities should still have the option for these important core courses that teach *real life*.

How are we supposed to know what the real world is like if we don't learn the fundamentals in high school or college? Who is going to teach us? Is it our parents? Our mentors? The world is much different than when they were growing up and entering the workforce.

When everything else in the world is evolving, why are so many of these prestigious universities with tenured professors remaining the same?

On whom do we feel we to have to rely in these times? None other than, you got it: **ourselves**! So of course we're self-entitled, self-reliant, self-absorbed, annoying twenty and thirty-somethings. That's how we were raised, that's how we got this far, and now we have been put in a position where we have no choice but to use it to our advantage.

We leave college thinking that it has had some great "grown up" effect on us and that all is well because our parents have raised us correctly, and while this may be true and our confidence is at an all-time high—*we still can't find a decent job*! Budget cuts, nepotism, whatever the reason may be—we're screwed. We spend countless hours sending hundreds of résumés online that go into cyberspace, never to even have one human eyeball glance over them.

In order to have all of our questions answered for this adulthood we weren't prepared for, we have little choice, but to exhaust the one resource we have learned to trust the most in life, Google. We Google: budgets, interview questions, résumé formats, proper business attire, and we piece together what we think will work best for us.

To play devil's advocate; say we do land a job at our dream company (probably because we had a summer internship with them) so we start out as an assistant. The minimum tenure we are going to spend as an assistant is two years, until being promoted to coordinator with a slight pay increase, then two to three years there before being promoted to manager (*maybe),* and so on. The corporate ladder takes foreverrrrrr (in our impatient eyes) to climb without some sort of God-given miracle nowadays!

When it comes to this notion that "hard work equals reward", as a generation, we cannot relate. That phrase went out the window the second we were given a graduation ceremony for finishing kindergarten and a trophy for just participating in (not winning) sports. Thank you helicopter parents (a term to describe parents who take an overprotective or excessive interest in the life of their children *especially* when it comes to education)!

Point being, working hard to get praise/success was not one of the virtues instilled in us. So yes, we do feel a bit entitled, and yes, we crave praise when we feel we're doing a good job. Honestly, we feel we deserve praise sometimes just for showing up!

Needless to say, the corporate world rains on our parade when it comes to all of the above and more so in the end, we are just really not interested in the slow ladder to nowhere.

Don't worry though; I'm done complaining and ranting about the corporate life because we have found the solution! Get ready...

We're all going to become entrepreneurs!

Absolutely nothing sounds more enticing to a Millennial than being their own boss! And so, it begins.... the apps, the websites, YouTube channels; technology extravaganza! We are going to create work for ourselves, even if during the beginning stages we don't receive much recognition or pay for our hard efforts. We are more determined than ever to make it work, because we're investing in ourselves and something we truly believe in—and this happens to be one of the only things *we do* have patience for! Oh, and did I mention we have no one to answer to, but ourselves? Yes, we've struck gold!

We will teach ourselves the ins and outs, and we will reap all the benefits of our trial and error mentality.

Sometimes this whimsical attitude means we're getting what some would call a "later start in life" since we won't have a stable job in the beginning, but that's NBD* to us. As I previously mentioned, many of us only have the obligation of taking care of ourselves at the moment, so as long as our needs are being met, we are not worried. We're keeping the faith that the success and money will come!

A majority of successful Millennials have stumbled upon their accomplishments just by following their passions and doing what they love.

A famous example: Mark Zuckerberg, billionaire, and founder of Facebook! Do you think his goal when creating Facebook was to become an overnight sensation? Nope. He was simply doing what he loved, breaking rules and writing code for a new program that was used as a tool for students to communicate.

Take a look at Evan Spiegel, co-founder and CEO of Snapchat, named 2015's youngest billionaire on the planet.

Daniel Fine, the founder of Glass-U, the folding sunglasses, who made Forbes 2016 "30 Under 30" list at the age of twenty-one.

The one thing all three of these success stories have in common is starting small at doing something they were passionate about and watching it transform into something the masses desired. These are only a few of the thousands of success stories of Millennials, but they drive the point home. It's inevitable that if you're pursuing something you enjoy—you will give it one-hundred and ten percent, ensuring its triumph.

Growing up, my father worked hard in the military, fourteen to sixteen-hour days a lot of the time, at jobs he wasn't always thrilled to be working.

Work/life combo took a toll on him. Even when he wasn't happy with work, quitting was absolutely not a choice, with a wife and two children depending on him as the sole bread winner (not to mention being obligated due to his commissioning with the U.S.

Army). It was something he didn't have the luxury of walking away from whenever he wanted. I know many of our parents dealt with the same issue.

Who knows how different our parents' lives would have been if they had the same endless possibilities as Millennials do.

From a Millennial's perspective, life wasn't meant to be enjoyed solely Friday evening through Sunday. The weekend is a stupid, man-made concept.

I'm not saying we shouldn't be disciplined; adhering to some sort of schedule. I'm saying why should we all have to succumb to society's timetable of a nine-to-five, forty-hour work week, or the idea of what a "grown up job" should look like? For some people, the nine-to-five may be doing what they love, and they have found their passion in that. That's perfectly fine. More power to you. However, the majority of us want to be our own boss and run our own empire. So, anyone who doesn't believe in what we're doing can go kick rocks!

It's all about striving to do what we love because we are social innovators and have realized the point of living and our reason for being is to be happy. More importantly, we have embraced the big idea of enlightenment in all of this: happiness is the overall goal.

Millennials will continue our search for a "work" life we are passionate about until we find it. Until then - call us lazy, call us entitled, call us whatever the hell you'd like, because honestly, we don't care what you think about us. We've got nothing to prove to anyone, but ourselves! We're one-hundred percent **unapologetic** for our attitude.

# ADULTING

# FOUR

This seems like a good topic to follow work life... let's talk about adulting*, specifically when it comes to our love lives, or the lack thereof. It's an intricate topic to dissect, so I've broken it down into four main categories: dating, marriage, having children, and Millennials as parentals*.

## Dating

Oh, the ups and downs of dating...and by that, I mean the lefts and rights of swiping ;).

Let me just start off by saying, this can be an extremely exhausting topic. However, the good news is - a single thirty-five year-old woman no longer has to be seen as the "lonely cat lady" my friends!

I think we can all agree that the way Millennials are dating today is one hundred and eighty degrees different from generations before.

The dating saga can be exhausting, but it can also be

exhilarating, and we Millennials take full advantage of this. We want to meet someone who is like-minded, enjoys life, and makes us want to be the best version of ourselves. The more people we date, the more we become an expert for what we feel is best for us. Through my numerous — and I do mean numerous/never-ending/continuous — encounters, conversations, and dates with guys, I can now tell within the first twenty minutes of meeting a guy whether I'm interested in investing any more of my time. Some of my red flags are in his initial first lines. If he asks anything similar to the following, it's not going to work out:

*I have plans with my friends tomorrow, but do you want to meet up afterwards when I leave the bar?* **No!**

*I'm not looking for anything serious, but we could always Netflix and chill?* **No!**

Bruhhhh please. Those may seem like obvious red flags, but you'd be surprised by how many girls give guys hall passes on these! Those types of questions indicate that he is not looking for the same thing that I am, so I will not waste his time, nor mine.

However, if he asks something along the lines of the following, chances are we're on the same page at least at the moment:

*Where's your favorite place to travel to?* **Italy**

*What are your hobbies outside of work?* **Happy Hour** *(no, seriously)*

*Are you close with your family?* **Yes**

The first set of questions tells me he's probably not

interested in anything past one night. The second set is much more genuine and comes from someone who seems interested in at least getting to know me and I could probably enjoy having good conversation over dinner or drinks and seeing where things go from there.

Sometimes, though, it's not simply that black and white. Whether the right questions are being asked or not, many of us still end up on those dates where we would rather chew our own arm off than finish dinner. So we throw out the one liner "OMG* my roommate just texted me and she's locked out so I have to leave to go let her in! Ok byeee!" C'ya never!

As innovative as we Millennials are, it's no surprise that we have come up with a solution and timesaver to help us avoid finding dates confined by four walls and a bartender: meaning only meeting someone at a bar one drunken night, although it does still happen that way from time to time.

The game changer? *Dating websites and apps!*

What better way to meet someone than swiping right and left on apps like Tinder, Hinge, or Bumble; being mutually attracted to each other, exchanging a few lines of conversation to test the waters, and ultimately deciding to grab a coffee or drink (or three). If it works, great, and if it doesn't—that's okay, too. We barely invested any time or money into the person at that point, so it's on to the next! These websites and apps are literally like catalog shopping for partners when you think about it.

> *He has a dog* – AWWW, *YESSSS.*
> *browses to the next *
> *Oh, he says he voted for Trump* – *HELL NOOOO!*
> *browses more*.

As shallow as that may seem, you can't argue that we are introduced to people we would have never met otherwise. It opens up doors for not only dating and a chance at finding true love, but friendships and networking as well. I personally know plenty of couples that have gotten engaged and married after meeting on a dating app, thanks to this new dating technology.

Dating sites have become trendy, a new part of social media. We're not embarrassed to be on them, in fact we embrace them. Millennials are truly fascinated with finding the easiest and most time-efficient ways to get things done, and hey, it works.

How does that old saying go? "If it ain't broke, don't fix it"? Yea that's **not** our motto. We believe things can always be improved; especially when it comes to making our personal lives easier on a daily basis.

This works great for us because as a generation, we put little time and effort into things that we're not passionate about (or at least not passionate about *yet*), even if it is another person. Simply swiping left and right based solely on a few pictures and a short bio? That is right up our alley!

While I talk about the greatness of dating websites, I'd be doing you all a disservice by failing to mention their biggest downfall: They make our options endless…and I do mean ENDLESS.

Raise your hand if you're in a city and you've swiped for hours!

While endless options in and of itself sounds amazing, it also encourages us to constantly be on the prowl for the better trade-up. Because, why settle, right?

Dating apps have also created some dishonesty and lack of trust when it comes to relationships. Being catfished* over and over, dick pics in circulation, and not to mention the brutal back-lash you receive if you're not receptive to this type of crude behavior. I also know a lot of people have found out that their "committed" boyfriend or girlfriend made an account on a dating website. When confronted, they insisted it was harmless, but that they just wanted to see what else was out there, to see who else out there finds them desirable.

That's a slow burnnn.

I've also been in a situation where I met a great guy on a dating site, we went on a few dates, decided it was worth pursuing so we both deleted our online accounts in front of each other as a "romantic gesture". Only about a month later we came across each other again on the *same* site we'd met on… while we were "exclusively" dating! HA! Busted. Needless to say, we had both reactivated our accounts. In this situation, who can be mad at whom? It just proved even though we both knew we had a good thing we were still *curious* to see what else may be out there and that's the truth.

This notion of never being satisfied has made a lot of solid relationships feel instantly disposable and made it hard to form those solid trusting relationships in the first place. Therefore, people are taking a lot longer to commit.

It all leads me to wonder, how long will this mindset of *onto the next* or *looking for the upgrade* last? Will it disintegrate with age? Or is it all about finding that one person who makes you feel like you have found the Holy Grail, and you don't even want to look elsewhere? Should we take our continuous curiosity as a sign that we have not found that person yet or that the timing is off? I was honestly not sure so I surveyed a group of peers on the topic and the results were pretty much inconclusive. Some people said they would stop when they found the right person. Others put down an age when they planned on actually settling down. Some said when they were more stable financially or more established in their careers and of course…some said when they were done having their fun. Interesting. I suppose only time will tell with that one.

Regardless, one dating rule that remains in place for Millennials is no one condones being cheated on or put on the back burner. Relationships are all about mutual respect and trust. Once either of those are compromised, you can be assured the relationship will start to tank... really quick.

To directly address the influence of the dating app on us; I think most confusion and distrust can be avoided if we are true to our feelings and honest with whoever we're dating. Tell the other person you're still shopping around, or that you are looking to commit. Just talk people -TALK!

The rest will eventually work itself out.

All things considered, while we may have become serial daters, we are no strangers to the satisfying drug of *love*. Ok that sounded corny AF*, but seriously...

Many of us still really do believe that true love exists. We have no choice, but to keep the faith that we will find it one day. After all, we have acknowledged that a big part of our happiness on this earth (which is the most important thing to us) is to love and to be loved.

Digging into the levels of dating for our generation, your twenties - thirties are a time to come into your own, to get to know the skin you're in, enjoy your youth and live it up and most importantly to learn to love yourself - alone!

It is a time to explore the world. What is it about life you appreciate and want to bring to the table in any relationship? There is so much greatness and so many amazing people all around us, and you will be crippling yourself for the future if you don't take advantage of this time to culture yourself, meet new people, and grow before you decide to settle down.

My overall take on things? Dating can be a drag, but it can also be an amazing opportunity to meet an abundance of diverse people and to get to know who you are, so you can tell the difference between Mr. Right and Mr. Right Now.

Then, when Mr. Right does come along you can spot him from a mile away and take hold of the situation without any apprehension or questioning.

If you haven't found that person yet, chin up—keep looking, you will. If you think you had that person and they got away, I'd try to get them back, and if you can't then keep it movin' with your head held high. That means they probably weren't the one, or the timing was off. If you are one of the lucky ones who found that person, lucky you. Love the shit out of them; Every. Single. Day.

A successful relationship really is all about knowing who you are, what you're looking for and then being ready when you find it - at that right time. The combination is magical AF*! Find your unicorn.

Oh and if you are one of the ones who has decided to remain single forever — Cheers to you too!


## MARRIAGE


So…it pains me to say, according to an article written by ABCNews, thirty years ago, ninety-five percent of all thirty-one year-old women had already tied the knot.

To clarify, those are pains of sadness for the women who never got to truly experience their freedom… I'm going to pour some champagne out for them. Lol, IM KIDDING (sort of). I don't waste champagne.

Fortunately, Millennials broke free from yet another societal stigma! We are unapologetically single AF* and living up our twenties AND thirties up!

The Washington Post reported, in 2016 the average age for marriage was twenty-seven for women and twenty-nine for men in America and in urban cities these ages were even *higher*. Most of us decided to hold off on the standard marriage right after college with kids directly following. There are many reasons for this decision, but let's discuss a few main ones.

First and foremost, we are the "divorce babies". Many of us are the children of divorced moms and dads. Most of our parents got married (what we would consider) too young, straight out of high school or college, and more or less "settled" into their current situation at the time. This landed over half of them in a divorce and most likely all of them in a mid-life crisis later on.

It needs to be said that *divorce* doesn't sit well with Millennials. It is something our generation is all too familiar with, despises, and hopes to avoid at all costs. And who can blame us? The divorce rates were the highest during our childhood into our teenage years compared to any previous generation. Therefore, so many of us grew up in single parent households. We split holidays, households and learned to love (or hate) step-parents and step-siblings. This had a huge impact on how we view relationships, marriage, and commitment in general. Most of us have decided to wait until our thirties to get married (which, in turn, drives our parents crazy)!

Although our parents may acknowledge they left us a bit ruined and with little faith in "forever" relationships; the mere thought that we will be single forever and never give them grandbabies scares the hell out of them! So, we get a little payback. Mwahaha…

However, everyone can chill out! Waiting is actually one of the smartest decisions we've made by far. By doing so, we get all of the partying, dating, and exploring out of our system, and by the time we begin to think about marriage, we are comfortable with ourselves, more established with our career and who we are, and look forward to the idea of it all. No one is pressuring us at that point and we feel like we're making the decision based on all the right reasons.

We're not about the "trial and error" marriage—we want to be sure that the person who we are committing to being with for the rest of our lives is a person we truly like for who they are and see them being the best addition possible to our lives. Marriage is definitely a compromise, but you shouldn't have to compromise about things like common interests, basic concepts and ideas on living life, and a mutual love and respect for one another—these should be givens in any healthy, lasting relationship.

Although I am not a divorce baby, the majority of my friends and peers are.

I watched so many of them deal with divorce growing up. One of my best friend's parents went through a divorce when we were in high school. Please tell me, how many of you can relate to this situation?! Her mom felt unfulfilled, her dad said he was bored in the relationship and had been for years. Her mom saw that he was not giving her enough attention; he spent more time at the bar than with his family. In turn, her mom had an on-going affair. Her parents stayed together for their kids as long as they could, but after the continuous infidelity and feelings of being undesired, they finally filed for divorce. Their family was destroyed, their home no longer a safe-haven, and they ended up despising each other, making the kids feel as if they needed to choose a side.

After all that, they were both attempting the single life, going out to local bars, trying to meet other singles their age, looking for someone who accepted the baggage of a messy divorce and two teenagers from a marriage that really should have ended a long time ago. To be honest, they were both depressed because sometimes the fresh new start that sounds so appealing isn't as great as you thought it would be at the age of forty-three.

This scenario is a common one. Many of our parents got so lost in their marriages due to the lack of knowledge about themselves. By the time they became middle-aged, they didn't know who they were outside of the marriage and children. They got married very young, before they had really gotten to know themselves, including knowing their own likes and dislikes. They lacked a lot of knowledge regarding self-love and expected the love of someone else to be enough, but to their surprise, it wasn't.

As most of us acknowledge, self-love is the most important love because you can't love someone else without first loving yourself (Namaste); Millennials being a tad bit selfish, have figured this out!

"Us first, others later" equals the best possible outcome in our Millennial minds. We, as a generation, are very direct and are becoming more aware of what we want. In turn, there are not as many mixed signals and signs of confusion flying around.

Once we have that self-love established, we have more than enough love to go around.

When it comes to waiting longer before getting married, this notion can seem scary because it's never been done before. We are essentially the pioneers building the foundation for this, but it's important we embrace it!

I know what you're thinking. I should *want* to be married since my parents were such great models of the "perfect couple" and are still together.

Well, my parents met in college in 1980. My mom told me that the second she saw my dad, an angel whispered in her ear, "that's the man you're going to marry." To be honest, do you know what I think whispered in her ear? *Lust.* My dad had his shirt off and was standing on his front porch. My mom was with a group of her friends—and I wonder how many other girls heard similar whispers in their ears?

In fact, I think I've heard whispers, too, like every time I saw Leonardo DiCaprio, Bradley Cooper, and the hot bartender down the street who gives me free drinks—*there's my husband!* Just kidding, mom! I'm not throwing shade* at my mother; I believe my mother heard or felt something.

My parents have been together for over thirty-five years now (claps all around). However, the controversial question at hand:

*Do I think my parents are each other's ideal match?*

No, I don't. I think they both could have found other partners out there that they would have been much more compatible with. Someone they would have fought with a lot less and not had to work as hard with at their marriage.

However, I do think where my parents excelled was in their commitment to each other. Through all the hard times when it would have been easier to give up, to get a divorce, they chose to stay, to continue to work at it and be the best parents possible! So even though in my eyes they may not be the picture of what an "ideal couple" looks like, they definitely showed me what it looks like to never give up on someone.

So, here's to thirty-five more years, you two! Prost*!

Before we go any further, I know there is no such thing as a *perfect* relationship, and I am not saying that Millennials are refusing to settle for anything less than perfect. What I am saying is that you cannot deny that waiting longer gives us a better understanding of who we really are as individuals. As well, being more established in our lives and careers means less fighting about money and every other thing. We want to escape the fighting and constant bickering, the arguments, the divorce and split households, the cheating and lying.

We learned from our parents' mistakes and we really

just want to be as happy as possible.

As far as soul mates go, I actually *do* believe that everyone has one. To me, a soul mate is that one other person who understands your thoughts without you expressing them, your feelings without you sharing them. They understand your heart and are ultimately the best match for you. Although I believe in the concept, I think less than 0.000001 percent of the population will ever meet or even come in contact with that person.

Who is to say that your soul mate lives in the same town, the same country, or even speaks the same language as you? Leading me to believe it's practically impossible to find and marry your *soul's* mate, but when it comes to finding someone you are extremely compatible with and can fall in love with, that is very doable.

In fact, there are now compatibility tests that tell you the levels of attraction, hobbies, ideas, ambitions, upbringing, and personality traits that mesh the best with yours—we now have tons of different ways to tell if we are companionable with another person. So, finding that person in life at the right time, *that* is the goal. I know I'm repeating this, but take careful note that timing really does play a huge part in this.

That is what we're all aiming for, to live happily ever after with someone we feel was meant for us. We rest assured that they will be well worth the wait! So, relax Moms and Dads… we may be taking just a little bit longer, but we got this.

## HAVING CHILDREN

Now with all this talk about waiting… *waiting* to meet the right one, *waiting* to marry, and *waiting* to have kids… let me address the elephant in the room.

*Exactly how long can we wait to do all of this?*

As I talk about growing up according to a pre-planned timetable, some of you ladies may only be hearing a tick-tock in your ear…the sound of a woman's biological clock ticking away. Let me first address what a biological clock is, and I'll start by telling you it is *not* an actual clock.

According to Women's Health and Fitness website, Professor Bill Ledger of obstetrics and gynecology at The Royal Hospital for Women and advisor to Clearblue says we mustn't confuse the medical guidelines regarding having a baby from a health and fertility point of view with the social phenomenon referred to as the "biological clock". He explains that it is true from a medical standpoint that the best ages to get pregnant fall between 20 and 35 years. This is because a woman is most fertile and least likely to have other complications between those ages.

However, this in no way puts an expiration date on our eggs on our thirty-fifth birthday, nor that a woman can't have a healthy pregnancy after. We are seeing more healthy pregnancies happen later and later in life. From a celeb stand point: According to NY Daily News, Halle Berry became pregnant at the age of forty-one and then again at forty-seven, delivering two healthy babies. Mariah Carey became a mother of twin babies at the age of forty-two. Gwen Stefani welcomed her third child at the age of forty-four. Tina Fey also had a baby at the age of forty-one.

Yes, it is a fair argument that many celebrities have monetary advantages that allow them to afford things such as In Vitro Fertilization (IVF) and the best healthcare.

However, while this may be true about celebrities, some of us also have personal friends who have chosen to have children later in life. For example, my friend Mary just had a healthy second pregnancy at age forty-one, and my previous boss had twins at the age of forty-three. The fact that we are living longer and taking better care of our bodies is a huge factor in all of this!

The main point I'm making is just knowing that there are options out there that can keep our biological clocks at bay and that these options are becoming more of the norm is advancement in itself.

I'm not suggesting we all want to wait until we're forty-five years old to start having kids, but the "standard" two kids by twenty-five (which was the norm back in the Fifties and Sixties) is definitely considered out-of-date and no longer necessary.


## MILLENNIALS AS PARENTALS

Let's discuss the portion of Millennials who have already started to have children. First of all, wow, what a different world these children are growing up in. The advancements all around obviously ensure a technology-based upbringing. Meaning, they are learning everything through a monitor screen. Whether it is a smart phone, iPad, or television – this is their teacher.

Moms are texting while "watching" their children; dads playing virtual baseball with their sons instead of the good old-fashioned bat and ball.

Who else has had a toddler show *you* how to turn on a video they wanted to watch because you were doing it too slow? These kids are already freaking smarter than the smart phones.

Granted a lot of these programs/videos they are watching can be considered educational; however, there's something to say about a different type of essential learning from peers and the real world that these videos do not offer.

What happened to "Go outside and play. Come

home when the street lights turn on." I honestly feel bad these kids will be missing out on that type of childhood. Although it seems impossible, I do encourage Millennial parents to put an effort into making their children go play with sticks, draw with chalk, jump rope, all the oldies but goodies we did to entertain ourselves. I truly do not think this technology overload will be healthy for them in the long run. I for one do not want my child to know how to connect with an iPad more than a person.

I can already see educational institutions being replaced by online programs for grade school. It's going to be a robotic world.

But yes, I must say, it's great when we're at a restaurant and my nephew is screaming at the top of his lungs and all we need to do is put on the ABC video for him to watch and keep quiet. However, that can't always be the solution.

We're going to have to find a way to balance out the videos with playing outside. As we already know, technology isn't going anywhere, there's no running from it. Nevertheless, we can try to keep it at somewhat of a distance from our children while we raise them.

To be honest, I'm torn on this topic. I'm one hundred percent for tech advancement, since that has become part of my generation's DNA. However, I would be lying if I did not address the concerns it brings along with it. I want my children to grow up with humanistic communication skills and I want them to still feel independent when disconnected from a smart device. The majority of us cannot put our phone down for five minutes. So, what do you think we are teaching these children? I have a solid argument that Millennials are still great with face-to-face communication despite our technology upbringing. However, if technology is all these kids are ever exposed to, I'm not sure I will be able to make the same argument.

As parents, we are going to have to be aware and conscious of the situation at hand. We are going to have to really keep up with technology in order to set limitations and boundaries for this new generation. We are going to have to know how to use the most up to date blocking and monitoring software in order to maintain a safe and stable upbringing.

Millennials have joked about our parents' lack of knowledge regarding technology and how long they take to catch on to the newest tech trends. Millennials as parents are simply not going to have that luxury. We are going to have to keep pace ensuring that we are still the ones raising our children and not a computer.

However, maybe our children will be able to handle this phenomenon better than we think considering it is all they will have ever known. Maybe they won't be as crazed by technology as we were. Wouldn't that be a relief for all of us!

I know Millennials are going to be very supportive, loving and driven parents. They are going to raise their children to be dreamers. Aside from that - as this new generation known as Gen Z (and the ones to follow shortly) get older, I'm not sure exactly what we can expect from them, but it's up to us to show them how to sift through this newly created tech world.

Overall, to wrap the chapter up, whether you agree or not with the Millennial take on dating, marriage, having children, and how we'll be raising them; a copious amount of studies tell us waiting and taking our time when it comes to relationships and starting a family is okay. Don't force it.

If it is something you're desperately looking for, put yourself out there and eventually I'm sure it will come to you, but there's no need to be embarrassed or try to rush into something just because you aren't falling into the category of society's "norm".

Breaking news: *WE ARE the new norm!*

# Our *Spiritual* Journey

# FIVE

Spiritual—religious—agnostic—atheist. Whatever you "label" yourself; most Millennials were raised with some type of religious influence. This mostly consisted of church, temple, mosque, Sunday school, maybe a youth group in junior high, even attending a Christian school and weekend bar/bat mitzvahs. But looking back I wonder, what did this mean to all of us growing up?

At the time, I don't think any of us were quite sure. We knew it was what we were supposed to do, it was what we were *told* to do, what we were conditioned to do.

Everything religious seemed to feel very ritualistic to most of us; over half the time in church we spent drawing or coloring, playing with our Nanos, Giga Pets, or Gameboys – anything that our parents would allow in order to keep us occupied and more importantly, quiet. It felt like most of the sermons never really clicked with us, but we knew to give thanks for everything positive in our lives and graciously ask for things we wanted.

As we got older we started to ask questions about religion; questions that a lot of our parents and peers couldn't explain. We felt guilty for having these feelings of doubt, but it just didn't feel right believing in something that we couldn't quite understand. Just *having* faith didn't seem to be enough when it came to an entire book or story we were told to believe in but could not comprehend. This isn't to say that Millennials turned atheists, it's just that we started to feel comfortable enough as we got older to push the envelope on religion the same way we do with everything else.

In fact, it has been stated by Dr. Michael Hout, a professor of Sociology at NYU, who is well-versed in generational and religious changes in the United States, that:

*"Many Millennials have parents who are Baby Boomers, and Boomers expressed to their children that it's important to think for themselves—that they find their own moral compass. Also, they rejected the idea that a good kid is an obedient kid. That's at odds with organizations, like churches, that have a long tradition of official teaching and obedience. And more than any other group, Millennials have been and are still being formed in this cultural context. As a result, they are more likely to have a 'do-it-yourself' attitude toward religion."[9]*

Millennials have taken it upon themselves to alter common religious practices into their own form of religion. If we pray, it's simply because it makes us feel better, but some of us stopped going to weekly religious services because we didn't like the structure. We began to look at our lives as a whole and become more spiritually aware of what we're doing here. As I stated many times before, Millennials just want to be happy; understanding the beliefs that guide our decision-making processes is a huge part of that happiness.

In general terms, many of us found peace with saying we're spiritual as opposed to religious. Many of my Jewish friends now identify as Jew-*ish*.

Sure, most Millennials believe in *a God* because we believe life isn't just a coincidence and whoever or whatever put us here deserves a name and praise for doing so, but we're not quite sure what's past that. Don't get me wrong, we're grateful; we're just not sure how to deal with all the unanswered questions and don't necessarily believe that going to church every Sunday makes us a good person.

Like I said, I was raised Christian, Lutheran to be specific. I was and still am proud to believe in God, but it's hard for me to invest too much past that. Does that mean I'm not a Christian because I'm not one-hundred percent sold on the Bible's teachings in its entirety? I'm actually not sure what that says about me. What I do know is that my life is focused around love, and isn't that what it's all about anyway? Loving one another, taking care of one another, helping one another, isn't that what religion is supposed to teach us? Not so much memorizing scripture, but applying peace, love, and faith into your everyday life. Jesus stated in Matthew 22:37-22:39 the second most important commandment to follow, after, "You shall love the Lord your God with all your heart, with all your soul, and with all your mind." is "Love your neighbor as yourself".

I've met some miserable Christians, some miserable Jews, and some miserable Atheists. This goes to show that it is not necessarily what your beliefs are, but how you act in your daily life. It always confuses me when people who have accepted religion into their way of life condemn others to Hell, or judge them negatively at all for that matter. It just doesn't seem very "religious" of them. I thought, "he who is without sin may cast the first stone"? And that means that no one is allowed to throw shit.

When you look at all of the blood that has been shed across generations because of religious wars, and different religious beliefs, even the way certain religions are discriminated against because of the way they dress… it's insane and unacceptable. Somewhere along the way they've missed the point. It makes Millennials want to turn away from all religious views because it isn't doing what it was intended to do—which is bring us all together, closer, as a people.

This is why I think religion and spirituality are very personal choices for everyone to make for themselves; maybe they find their peace through reading, meditation, singing, worship, writing, or praying. Whatever the case may be, I don't think attending multiple services you don't actually *want* to be at qualifies you as a religious person.

Personally, I found a church in LA that I go to on Wednesday nights, but it's the farthest thing from what I remember "church" being while I was growing up. It's also quite sad that we allow our definition of church to have such a negative connotation, considering the definition of a church according to Webster is a, "building for public and especially Christian worship." Meaning anywhere worship is happening can be considered a church. Yet, many of us only remember a church as a stuffy place where we had to sit still and behave ourselves for an hour or more.

The church I attend is different because it is not stuffy and uptight and I can actually relate to the messages. Our pastor, Judah Smith, is amazing! He's also quite hilarious which is a total bonus. Somehow every message delivered feels so personal and that's what it's about to me, having a personal relationship with God, one that has value and meaning to me and is not judged by others. However, if I hadn't found this church, I probably wouldn't be attending any at all at this moment in my life, because like everything else – I was looking for the right fit. Luckily, I found it.

Overall, I don't think any of us have right or wrong answers when it comes to the subject of religion, and I'm the last person to get into a religious debate . I have different views from my sister, and she has different views from my parents; it doesn't mean we can't all get past our personal religious ideas and love one another.

My philosophy with church has always been, "to each his own".

What I can say is that I feel it is very beneficial for us to have some type of faith in our lives, whether it is one-hundred percent religious-based or not. I believe faith to be one of the most important virtues.

Faith is the foundation in which we all build our lives on. Faith that we have a purpose, faith in mankind, faith that it's all going to work itself out. Faith is where it all starts.

In the end, your spiritual feelings and being are your prerogative, but I truly believe that it helps with your overall happiness to have faith in something. If we all had this common ground, I think the world would be a better place to live in. With faith comes a lot of other virtues (love, joy, peace, kindness) that make our existence so great to be a part of!

With that being said—search on. I find my spiritual and religious views to be constantly evolving as I continue my personal quest and education. I love reading new materials, hearing new ideas and notions, and making my religion personalized to me. I don't care what others think about my views. I have faith that I'm good with the Higher Power, and I'm good with myself; that is all I need to be concerned about. Your religious views can be as personal as you would like to make them and no one has the right to judge you for it — as you don't have that right, either.

I believe religion can be seen as a man-made concept, so personalize it to fit your own values, just as long as it all comes back to love for mankind.

# QUARTER-LIFE *CRISIS*

# SIX

The New Age concept of a quarter-life crisis is not to be confused with the definition of a mid-life crisis. We are probably all familiar with the term mid-life crisis. Webster's dictionary defines a mid-life crisis as, "a period of psychological stress occurring in middle age [forty-sixty years old], thought to be triggered by a physical, occupational, or domestic event such as menopause, diminution of physical prowess, job loss, or departure of children from the home."

Well, you know all that innovative stuff I keep talking about with us Millennials? Blah, blah, blah…. Here's to another term that was coined, one that's more efficient and exclusive to current Millennials: *quarter-life crisis*.

A quarter-life crisis, according to Forbes, usually happens in your mid twenties to early thirties, much sooner than the better-known mid-life crisis. It is a period in which a person begins to feel doubtful about their life, brought on by the stress of becoming an adult. Typically, because you're feeling you're not reaching your full potential or you're falling behind.

One day we wake up and realize we *are not* where we thought we would be after a quarter century of life. When we were teenagers, those four years of high school seemed to last *forever*, so we figured life would drag out like that as well. twenty-five seemed so far away. We figured ten years was equivalent to a century, and we'd definitely have it all together by then: the dream job, life partner, pool of money to swim in, and core group of friends to hang out with. However, twenty-five came out of nowhere like a slap in the face, and we didn't feel like, what society calls "grown-ups" at all. Next comes thirties. Damn, we were seriously not ready for this! *"So, no one told you life was gonna be this way…"*

But the difference between a quarter-life crisis and a mid-life crisis (besides the obvious fact that most of our wallets don't allow us to go out and buy a Corvette convertible at twenty-five) is that we aren't looking back on anything regretfully, we're not questioning past decisions and regretting things we can't change. We're dealing with the present and looking towards the future and where we should go from here. Yes, this is still scary AF*, but it is also much more proactive!

We talk to ourselves, we question what more we can do to make ourselves happy, to feel more fulfilled. We say things like, *"I don't like where I live. I should move!"*

*"I seriously hate this job! I'm going to quit and start looking for another one."*

*"I don't see this relationship going anywhere. I'm going to break it off and see what else the dating market has to offer."*

We literally question everything and try to make quick decisions accordingly.

I used to spend what felt like countless hours trying to figure out where I saw myself in five years, in ten years. After all, that's what people want to know isn't it?

Where do you see yourself ending up and what's your plan to get there?

With all this chaos going on in your mind, you re-evaluate what you even wanted in the first place and if you still crave that dream, if you think it's still worth the pursuit. Or if it's time to move on to something new and make changes.

No matter what your goals may be, in order to take the right steps, you mentally decide that you must have your priorities in order.

1) Career   2) Family   3) Friends   4) Dating

Wait, no…

1) Family   2) Career   3) Dating   4) Friends

Nah, still not right…

Your priority list continues to change as your focus shifts, and you wonder if each plant you potted is getting its share of nourishment, because you don't really see that part of your life flourishing as you had imagined.

To be honest, it's all a hot mess* upstairs. We try to make sense of it, but with no concrete answers at hand, what's the first thing we do? The worst thing possible? We compare!

We compare ourselves to our role models, to our friends, to our parents, to *anyone* we deem worth comparing. All of their timelines are different as well, which leaves us with… well, nothing!

Back and forth we go, scrimmaging with our minds.

*"Well, statistically I'm above the curve, but comparatively I think I'm behind."*

Because we play this tennis match with ourselves we are left confused. Sometimes feeling like we are letting others or ourselves down.

We're left exhausted and somewhat discouraged as we start the thinking process all over. Yet through this process we somehow gain a little bit more ambition, perspective and drive than we had before.

The good news in all of this my friends: *We're all in the same damn boat!*

We are all constantly changing our minds and shifting our energy in hope of finding what ultimately makes us happy, but our paths are not comparable with anyone else because our generation is just plain *different*.

Take a look at our parents for example. Most of them didn't understand what following their dreams meant because to them, the ultimate dream was instilled in being able to retire a little early and enjoy their 401k and social security benefits. Their "dream" was to have security. They simply don't get what we're struggling with. Our parents were conditioned to do what they saw as the responsible and safe thing.

However, this is not to say that previous generations were totally compliant and did not take any risk toward cultural advancements. In fact, they helped lay the overall foundation for change when it came to race equality, gender equality, gay rights – all those things we're still fighting for today and have made major advancements within, would not be nearly as far along if they had not used their voices.

A select few of our parents may have even experienced a quarter-life crisis themselves—but even if they did, most of them had no way to recognize it or what to call it, so it was dismissed instead of addressed as they carried on. This in turn, left them to succumb to their mid-life crisis.

To bring things home a bit and firmly address a part of my quarter life crisis, a quick personal story.

I had an epiphany while my parents were out in Los Angeles visiting me. We met up with some of my friends, and my parents had sponsored us all on a few bottles of wine, so everyone was feeling pretty relaxed that evening.

Exactly how it all started I don't recall, but what I do remember, and will never forget is this... I remember the bartender giving me a free drink and then being told by my mother that I had had enough.

"I'm 26 years old!" I exclaimed. "I'm an adult. I know my own limit".

My dad turned to me, and what he said next had nothing to do with my free drink or even the drunken situation at hand.

"When I was twenty-six, I was a Captain in the United States Army," he stated matter-of-factly. "What are *you* doing with your life?"

My heart sank into my stomach. I was in shock and for the first time I can remember, I literally had no words for him. It immediately felt as if I had been betrayed. I thought this whole time when he'd been telling me how proud of me he was for living in LA, for taking a risk and pursuing my dreams, that he meant it, yet now it seemed like it was all a lie.

*He doesn't think I'm doing anything,* I thought. *He thinks I'm just out here wasting time, wasting my life away.*

I wondered how long he'd been waiting to say those words to me. I got up and left and went back to my apartment, leaving my parents at their hotel.

I had never in my entire life felt like I let my dad down as much as I did in that one moment.

How could he not see how hard I was working? How much I was doing to make my own dreams come true, all while still paying my own bills on time? Don't I get any credit?

That conversation was never brought up again. It weighed heavily with me for some time, and then all of a sudden, after months of dwelling on the situation, it clicked.

It wasn't that he wasn't proud or was being self-righteous; it was simply that *he didn't get it.*

He honestly and truly doesn't understand what I'm trying to do. He is scared for me and yearns for some type of security *for me.*

To my dad, having that nine-to-five job with benefits means security, and while I'm out here pursuing my television hosting career, going through my quarter life-crisis, I don't have that security. I'm going from one audition to the next in this cutthroat town, being ridiculed, used, compared, and lied to. Yet, I still go at it because my dreams are what matter to me—meanwhile, all my dad can see is that I don't have future security and he's scared for me.

I'll be honest— when he first said this to me, not only was I crushed, but my quarter-life crisis mode kicked in, and I contemplated: *Maybe he's right. Maybe I'm wasting my time. Maybe I should move or pursue a different career.* Then I realized – nope he's wrong. Pursuing the life you want is *never* a waste of time. You will only ever regret what you never tried to do.

At that age of twenty-six he was married and my older sister had already been born. He had a family to provide for. He didn't have the luxury of figuring out what he really wanted to do with his life. His father had been in the military before him for over thirty years, so that was what he knew. For my father, that career meant security.

At that moment of realization, I decided not to take it personally and to forgive his words. I decided that he didn't have to understand or approve of what I was trying to do, and honestly, I still don't expect him or anyone else to. I am on this journey for myself, so as long as I'm okay with it, then that's all that matters. I know my parents love me and that's all I need from them – their love.

A couple years ago I watched Jim Carrey's commencement speech to Maharishi University on YouTube, which absolutely blew my mind! He talked about growing up and taking chances; specifically taking a chance on faith. He told a short story about how his father could have been a great comedian, but instead his father was scared and took a safe job as an accountant. When Jim was twelve that "safe job" let his father go, and the family was forced to survive however they could. What Jim Carey said next is something I will never forget; he said the most important thing he learned from the situation was that "you can fail at what you don't want, so you might as well take a chance on doing what you love!"[10]

Millennials: Look at the quarter-life crisis as a kick in the ass to get moving! What else could you be doing that you're not? What other steps could you take? While this can be a very frustrating time for us as we evaluate our lives up to this point, it is important to take this crisis as a chance to re-evaluate our goals and put an action plan in place to make them happen!

I'm predicting a mid-life crisis is probably something many Millennials will never experience. Why? Because we recognized our quarter-life crisis and got it all out of our system! We decided 45-50 years old was too long to wait to evaluate our life situation. Why would you want to have a nervous breakdown in the MIDDLE of your life? *No thanks!* We'd rather get it out of the way now as we figure out which direction we want to take on our incredible journey!

I have come to realize that trying to figure out *what you want* and *where you see yourself* in the future isn't constructive— what's constructive is figuring out how to live in the present moment, while life happens, and you'll get to where you're supposed to be.

Have some peace of mind that it's going to all work out!

# LAW OF ATTRACTION

# SEVEN

I think by now we've all heard that statistic Forbes reported regarding one percent of the population owning half of the world's wealth. Why do you think that is? Is this a coincidence or a conspiracy perhaps? Maybe that's what you believe, but I don't. I believe it's simply because the one percent uses this combination of faith and the Law of Attraction each and every day. Successful people expect that something good is on the horizon while working to make it happen.

I wanted to touch on this topic because it has been a tool I have used in my life ever since I learned about it in 2012 after reading The Secret, which I highly recommend for people getting started and just learning about this subject. By definition, the Law of Attraction is a magnetic power that manifests through your thoughts, by drawing to you, thoughts and ideas of a similar kind. What you think is what you get.

This can be a very exciting yet scary concept. The Law of Attraction was practiced by many successful people, including Albert Einstein, Henry Ford, Jim Carrey, and Steve Jobs. Good or bad, your thoughts attract everything in your life. It is becoming a common idea understood by many Millennials.

Have you ever thought about something over and over again and then "coincidentally" it happened and you said to yourself, *"I knew that was going to happen!"* Well of course you did, because you validated it as a real experience. Many Millennials use this idea during and around their quarter-life crisis to help guide them to their true calling. We have discovered the power of this law very early in life and use it to our advantage in every single way.

The Law of Attraction takes everything a step further and not only holds you accountable for your actions, but your *thoughts* as well. It's amazing to think we have such a life-altering power, but it can be hard to accept that we've created a lot of our exterior circumstances. You may not believe this to be true, but if you take the time and look back on your life and throughout history, you will see plenty of examples.

I have one that goes all the way back to my childhood.

This would be insignificant information except for the fact that it was the first time I looked back and saw the Law of Attraction had come into play. I want you to see just how authentic and strong it is.

I remember living in North Carolina when I was eight years old and telling my mom I had decided I wanted to become Amish. Yes, Amish. The people who live with no electricity and use a horse and buggy for transportation. I had never lived near any Amish people, but my grandparents lived in Newville,

Pennsylvania where my mother had grown up, and I would always see the Amish when I went to visit.

We went to their farmer's markets and bought their bread, fruit, and whoopie pies (AKA crack pies, if you've had one you know what I'm talking about). My mom asked me why I wanted to be Amish, and I told her I wanted the "simple life," whatever that meant to an eight-year-old. She falsely and lovingly entertained my idea and told me that was fine, but I had to go to college first.

I agreed with her and asked her what a good college in Pennsylvania was so I could start my Amish life directly following graduation. She responded with Penn State. I had never heard of it and neither she nor my dad had gone there, but I valued her opinion very much.

"Great! That is where I'm going to go to college, and then I will become Amish!"

It's really funny how things turn out.

Although I lost the desire to become Amish, I never lost the desire to go to Penn State, a college whose campus I had never even set foot on.

After continuing to move with the military and then living in Germany for two years, randomly my father accepted his last position before retirement as the Professor of Military Science for ROTC at Penn State University. *MIND BLOWN!*

I knew it was much more than coincidence. I had attracted this into my life! When you believe in something as if it is already real, the world has no choice but to align the stars and give you what you want.

To be honest, had my dad not been stationed there, there's absolutely no way I would have been able to go to Penn State. My grades weren't that great, and I wouldn't have been able to afford out-of-state tuition. Thankfully, being a local resident of the town made it all possible. The only real "work" I needed to do was to expect it was going to happen and not worry how, just trust that it would.

Look back on your life and look for specific patterns, think of those things that you dwell on and end up happening; both good and bad.

Look at relationships and specific dating patterns: dating the same type of woman or man over and over again. Why is it that you get cheated on in every single relationship, yet your best friend always dates the best guys/girls who treat them so well? Well, it's because that's what you expect. You expect to get cheated on so the universe has no choice but to give you what you're telling it.

On the other hand, did you end up with your dream woman or man? The person you felt was made for you and you had thought about over and over. You couldn't figure out when or how it was going to happen, but you knew it was and then it did.

Do you see where I'm going with this?

All you have to do is stay focused and expect that the blessings are coming, constantly sending out positive vibes.

However, once you accept this as truth you also accept the responsibility to be in control of your thoughts. When I first heard this, I felt sick to my stomach and thought, *"Oh my gosh, not only do I have to monitor my mouth, but now my thoughts as well?!"*

Every time I had a bad thought I was scared it was going to come true. However, I learned that's not the case. You have the power to monitor your thoughts so when you start to think of a negative one, immediately change your frequencies to a positive one.

You might think this is impossible, and I'm not saying it's easy, you have to practice every single day. Start small and aim big. You will be surprised at how fast your life will change in every category you decide to apply it to.

You want more money? Do what many people have attested to; write yourself a check for the amount you want and believe you already have it!

The law works in miraculous ways and it is something we Millennials truly trust as a guiding light. It is especially important during our quarter-life crisis years. The Law of Attraction provides a specific guidance to us, which resonates with how we grew up thinking; I want it all.

By believing something great will happen, we are able to keep the fire in us burning and prevail with confidence in all our ventures, big or small.

As I stated, many of our successful one-percenters have figured this out and have applied it to their lives. Trust me, the only ingredient going into their success isn't just hard-work, it's thinking and believing success is going to happen. There are a lot of hard workers out there with three jobs that are still broke because they haven't discovered this power yet. They never reach their full potential. So why not take advantage of this free universal gift?

Read _The Secret_, written by Rhonda Byrne in 2006, as a starting guide for a more in-depth explanation and see for yourself.

Living your best life with success in mind.

# SOCIAL INNOVATORS

# EIGHT

As mentioned previously, the most influence we have on society today is through social media. Nowadays everything is a click away and we, the Millennials, are to thank (or blame lol depending on how you look at it). We demanded a world be created that no one thought possible. A world where you can instantly find basically anyone you were sure you'd never be in contact with again. A world where you can order an item online and have it show up at your door the same day. A world where you can launch your own television series regarding your thoughts on absolutely anything (or nothing) thanks to YouTube, Vimeo, etc.

We live in a world where you can meet your perfect partner within a 20-mile radius via Match, Tinder, Bumble, and Coffee Meets Bagel. But wait, want to find your "type" based on lifestyle, sexual preference, religion or race? Try Christian Mingle, Grindr, Jew Date, Black People Meet, or Farmers Meet. Yup, there's literally a cup of tea for everyone!

We now have the ability to not only communicate with people across the globe, but to talk with untouchable idols and celebrities we thought we'd never have access to via Twitter or Instagram.

This takes the concept of *six degrees of separation* to a whole new level; we've now scaled back to one or two degrees of separation from a distant six. These social media sites I named are some of the most popular, but are only a *few* of the thousands out there and that we are constantly growing with. Every other person I meet is creating some type of app or at least thinks they have the *best idea* for one. Now I know some people think a lot of these social media apps can be a complete waste of time; not to mention very pretentious and self-centered.

However, not all Millennial-inspired apps or websites are just for dating and meeting new/old friends. Recently we've seen an increase in fundraiser apps/websites that have enabled us to help others that are struggling financially or need some investors.

One of my high school classmates had a dog that got cancer and the back leg needed to be amputated or else the dog was going to die. The doctor said the dog would easily adjust to having three legs, so that wasn't the problem; the problem was money, or lack of it. My friend couldn't afford the $3,000 operation. Just as all hope seemed lost, a friend recommended GoFundMe—a site used to launch ideas, projects, and fundraisers in hopes anyone was willing to donate.

Do you think he raised the $3,000? *Of course, he did!* All of us social media users, even those who were strangers, were not about to let that poor puppy die! That is just one example of the positive impact of these websites. They allow for the help of good Samaritans.

Another one; a pastor died in a car accident and left a wife and six kids behind. Immediately, an account was set up that raised hundreds of thousands of dollars to help support the family in the future. Celebrities were tweeting about it and entertainment news was covering it. What would have been a local newspaper story a decade ago turned into a national affair.

It is truly amazing how media not only has the ability to bring awareness, but can now give others the resources to truly do good deeds, wherever they are.

Of course, as we know all too well, with the good must come some bad…

I must admit we have become virtual slaves to social media. We now have a word that should not exist: *selfie*. By definition a selfie *is a photograph that one has taken of oneself, typically with a smartphone or webcam and shared via social media*. Yes, this is a real thing that mankind never saw coming. We are going around taking selfies of ourselves everywhere doing regular every day activities. Never before has any generation so carefully documented and put on display everything they're NOT doing.

On Instagram, we have selfies drinking wine, selfies cooking dinner, selfies laying by the pool, selfies working out, selfies walking in the park, selfies with the #OOTD*, selfies sitting in a cab #cabchronicles. We even have created a selfie-stick in order to achieve that ideal angle. We also have attachments to get the perfect lighting! We are on selfie *overload*.

We are so self-absorbed and we really think people care about what we're doing on a moment-to-moment basis. But wait… do they? How do we know if they care or not? *Count the likes!*

We are now measuring our entire existence and self-worth in correlation to how many followers we have, how many likes each Instagram picture gets or retweets we receive. In essence, how many people give a shit

91

about what you're doing (or most likely **not** doing) daily. It is pretty pathetic, yet something we are weirdly proud of it.

These types of social media sites are gold mines for gossip, cyber-stalking, and the main goal of course: becoming a social phenomenon. I have to admit I am guilty of succumbing to the selfie epidemic. In all honesty, selfies get way more attention or "likes" than any positive quote I post, which makes me kind of sad when I think about it.

However, our selfie pics are edited, they are so "filtered" and "saturated", that they're not even REAL.

An Australian model addressed this selfie epidemic and talked about how she got paid for every single item of clothing she wore or product she held or positioned in the background. Her half a million followers had become her self-esteem measure, and she had lost contact with **real people**, no longer talking with friends face-to-face and just being real.

She talked about her Instagram account becoming an addiction instead of a hobby, where she would take over five hundred pics to get "the right one". She ended up deleting her account in tribute to her twelve-year old self, whom she felt had been left behind when she started dreaming up all of this Insta-fame. To say the least, the message was powerful, truthful and emotional for many people.

What it really comes down to is that social media has become a vocal and visual platform for us all. We're comforted by the fact that it lets us have our voices heard, and we can showcase this image of having an amazing life; whether it's actually true or not, doesn't seem to matter.

We, as the human race, have always had a voice and an opinion, only now with social media we're no longer limited to telling our cats and dogs what we think while watching television—we're getting online and telling the entire world! Everyone gets to hear our rant or two-cents. It gives us the feeling of being a part of something much bigger than ourselves. We feel it gives us a greater purpose. It gives us a feeling of power.

It all started with the seemingly innocent old school social media crutches: AIM, Myspace, and then Facebook. While two of the three have faded out, Facebook remains strong. In college, it was used to help us connect with peers at our school, but now? It has become our electronic diary. We put all of our thoughts and feelings into a post and share it with our hundreds or thousands of "friends" to see.

*"Joe cheated on me… he is such a dick, but you bitches still need to mind your own business!"*

Or, *"I just found out I'm not my best friend's best friend… it sucks."*

This was posted by a twenty-nine year-old woman I am "friends" with who must still be stuck in middle school. It is absolutely ridiculous! Seriously, why would you even want the world to know some of the crazy shit you're thinking? Your mouth is meant to be a filter for your thoughts, but now we can express everything through a keyboard in a matter of seconds without uttering a sound. Giving us zero time to *think before we tweet*\*.

With reality shows booming and people getting a real insight into other's lives (like the infamous Kardashians), airing our dirty laundry has become the norm. We no longer feel the need to keep things to ourselves; we would rather get a reaction from the rest of the world.

Personally, I see why the Kardashians do it—they get paid millions for people to judge them. Hellooo sign me up! But aside from them, why would you *want* people who are not involved in your daily life to know the struggles and obstacles you're facing, however real or delusional they may be? This is where I differ from the Millennial mindset. I am much more conservative or, dare I say, *mature,* when it comes to putting my personal life on blast.

Facebook was originally created as a networking tool and has transformed into an online journal of opinions constantly streaming and updating on your newsfeed, and honestly, there is always so much more negative being posted than positive. It's interesting for me to see some people I met in college having the most immature attitudes on trivial subjects or projecting their close-minded views onto others.

Seriously…*get your head out of your app* (you see what I did there? Lol).

It really does change your opinion of someone to see their true colors from behind a keyboard. A term coined for this is **keyboard courage**. This is basically people who express every single thought they have, good or bad, that they would normally never say to another human being if they were face to face, yet the plastic keys seem to empower them.

It's all good though. I have a solution for you obnoxious Facebook users or "friends" clogging up my newsfeed with nonsense.

*click* *Unfriend.*

One last thought on Facebook:

No, I do not want to play Candy Crush, so please stop inviting me. Surely, I can't be the only person on Earth who finds matching candies and soda pop as a complete waste of time? Oh, I am? Ok then…lol!

Whether it's Snapchat, Facebook, Instagram, or Twitter, these types of social media sites aren't going away anytime soon. In fact, they are just the beginning. While these vocal and visual stages can be used for so much good, it is not the case the majority of the time. We are on social media overload.

However, I truly believe that we can change this pattern. We need to continue to build on these as a forum for networking and sharing valuable information, but we must proceed with caution when deciding how we use them and how we react to them. It is much easier said than done, I know, but it is possible.

Actually, BRB* I'm about to go update my profile pic... ; )

# A New *Dynasty*

# NINE

A generation of global pioneers has arrived. As stated in the previous chapter, Millennials evolved the way people meet and communicate. We grew up with programs that connect us, and now as grownups, we continue to find advancements for websites and programs like those that raised us.

Our network is larger than any before us; we connect with each other through plastic keys. Writing letters became outdated, and we craved more instant gratification. We made friends with people living across the country. We crushed over peers who we had never met. Who else had a Myspace boyfriend/girlfriend? And who else got catfished*?

We found people who we could relate to outside of school. They became our true friends! We were no longer limited to the assigned classroom of 24 students.

We spent countless hours sitting in front of the computer exchanging instant messages with complete strangers, sending pictures, and creating acronyms that took our parents years to decrypt: POS, LMAO, SMH, LOL, TTYL, CTFU (*)—just to name a few.

Through technology, we created a language that represented our generation early; we are original, and we have no time (not even enough time to spell out entire words). No time… and no patience. With technology, we made the impossible possible. For example, search engines reduce the need for feuded debates as to who is right or wrong over a factual matter; we simply take one minute and look it up! It's that easy.

There is absolutely no information that isn't within the grasps of a smartphone or keyboard.

Take a moment just to rethink how much technology has changed all of our daily activities. We no longer need a map to figure out where we're going; in fact, we can go to the same location one-hundred times, and we don't even need to retain the information on how to get there. With phone apps like Google Maps, Waze, or Hopstop, we will always get the fastest, most up-to-date route that accounts for traffic, accidents, construction, and train delays. Thus, we may take twenty different routes over time going to the exact same place just to save a few minutes—sadly, not remembering even ONE of those routes for future use!

We no longer need recipe books, and, if we forget how to cook something, there's no need to call mom to figure out how she makes her infamous banana bread.

In fact, we are more likely to look on Pinterest and find an even tastier, healthier and more time-efficient way to cook our favorite meals. There are now "expert" bloggers that have all of this covered. Not to mention it's completely free.

Even when it comes to being sick or wondering

what your specific symptoms mean, you no longer need to run to see a doctor. You can search on medical sites to find out what could possibly be wrong with you. Although, *user beware*, because even a simple search for "paper cut" seems to somehow lead back to some fatal illness! Lol*...no but really...it does. Everyone has a Web MD degree these days.

Technology has simplified so many situations that it would be difficult—actually impossible—for Millennials to imagine life without it. Has anyone else had a similar conversation with their parents to this one?

**MILLENIAL**: If you didn't have a cell phone then how did you make plans with friends?

**PARENT**: We called their landline.

**MILLENIAL**: Ok, I remember those, but what if they weren't home or didn't answer? You obviously couldn't text them.

**PARENT**: We called again later or left a message with whoever answered and waited for a call back.

**MILLENIAL**: Ok I get it, but how did you meet up once you made plans? What if they were running late? What if you got lost or stuck in traffic? What if they never showed up? How would you ever know any of this?!

**PARENT:** Well, surprisingly, that didn't happen much in our generation—but you would wait a standard thirty minutes like a normal person and then leave if they didn't show.

**MILLENIAL**: Wow—it must have been really hard for you growing up… I'm sorry.

This conversation is comedy, but true. In all seriousness, technology has taken the guessing game out of the equation for the most part. All information is available with the click of a button or the touch surface of a smartphone. All of this makes me wonder the absurd questions the next generation will be asking us as technology continues to progress. Probably something like:

"So, wait, you actually had to *drive* your own car? Hands on the steering wheel, foot on the gas?!"

Yuppp it'll be crazy AF*, and I can't wait!

With how amazing I've said the internet is, it has also caused problems that never occurred before its existence. Duh.

Through the Internet we were introduced to a concept called "cyberbullying" which also ties into the keyboard courage theory mentioned earlier. Although this topic diverts a little from technology it is directly linked to it.

Who would have thought the saying "sticks and stones will break my bones, but words will never hurt me" would turn to shit so fast? People started committing suicide as a result of these words being written *over a fucking keyboard*!

Previous generations dealt with face-to-face verbal abuse, but now, through technology, we unknowingly entered an entirely different universal realm. We are now subject to daily abuse by people who may have never even met us. No one is exempt from it either. Celebrities, political figures, the Pope, the most popular girl in school, and the class nerd; they are all subjected to this brutal treatment.

The power of words has become so real, and the internet has given everyone a voice. People who were powerless before have now found a form of power, a power that is all too easy to abuse. It's easy to tell someone you wish they would die or how fat and ugly they are when they're not standing in front of you for you to see the hurt you've caused. Somehow people think this form of bullying is *more* acceptable.

Khloe Kardashian tweeted out that she had been a major victim of cyberbullying. A well-known celebrity blogger had bullied her about her weight and looks for years bringing her to hysterical tears many times. This type of bullying can lead to detrimental behavior, not to mention major depression and eventually suicide.

Girls who get called fat may become bulimic or anorexic, boys who get called gay or faggot may go into a deep depression and don't feel they belong anywhere so they end it. People sharing nudes on the norm, seemingly without the understanding that once you send them into cyberspace, they are there to stay! This type of blackmail is definitely a new phenomenon.

We've also seen the very extreme cases of school shootings where people left messages on the internet, using it as a public platform, regarding how they were going to get revenge. Alongside this notion, horrific incidents such as these are more often than not carried out by people who felt like outcasts or had been severely bullied/cyberbullied themselves[8].

I learned early on the effects of cyberbullying and, even today am still subjected to it through some of the comments left on my web videos. Although I've tried to equip myself with tools to let it go instead of feed into it, I was only able to gain these tools by going through some emotional pain.

I'll never forget my first instance of being cyberbullied. I was twelve years old, in seventh grade when a boy in my class had sent me an email and asked me to be his girlfriend. I responded "no thank you" as I wasn't interested.

After feeling rejected he began to torment me every single day, and all of the sudden I "became" fat and ugly. I had never even *thought* about my weight before the age of twelve. *Was I fat?* I received Instant Messages from all of his friends telling me the same thing. It was like I couldn't escape the torture at school or when I was at home. I spent many nights crying myself to sleep.

One day at school I decided to stick up for myself.

"Shut up!" I yelled back in the middle of class as he taunted me about my weight in front of everyone. He came over to me and stood above my chair. He balled up his fist and punched me right in the side of my face as hard as he could.

That was the worst pain I ever remember experiencing up to that point. My eyes went black, and I saw stars. The teacher stood there with her jaw on the floor, which pretty much mimicked the rest of the class' reaction. After a few seconds (which seemed like hours) I came to and sat there in shock as my vision came back. I tried to figure out what had just happened. Then screamed and ran out of the class.

Nothing was broken, but there was a fracture, which the doctor said would heal on its own. I carried a huge bruise on my left cheek for over two and a half weeks. I realized that while the physical pain eventually went away, the emotional pain never quite did. The cyberbullying got worse, and shortly after that incident I was also tormented with a new name, fat *cry baby*.

Schools really didn't know how to deal with out-of-the-classroom cyberbullying since they had never seen it before. He was suspended for one week and that was it. However, what I realized was that words on a screen could hurt more than a punch in the face... literally.

People need to wake up and realize their actions on a computer are nothing to be taken lightly. Only then will this plague called cyberbullying subside. This is something our generation needs to own and alter in order to teach the next generations how to do better. Done and done.

Now, continuing on with technology and instant gratification conditioning our patience levels, let's scratch the surface on the subject of texting. *Whoa... the floodgates have opened!*

We live in a generation where an unanswered text literally triggers an anxiety attack. We get to know people through basic words, and we misinterpret half of what each other's texts mean anyway.

*I didn't like the TONE they had in that text message.*

But it's a great convenience to be able to think about what we want to say before we say it and even to respond on our own time. We see calling as an inconvenience—we have to stop what we are doing, pick up the phone, and focus all of our attention on what the other person is saying, and if we don't, we're considered rude; this is *agonizing* for us.

In a world where I'm busy and you're busy, multitasking is the norm, and we simply don't feel we have the time for long phone conversations. A basic text conversation can continue throughout the day, lasting for hours, whereas if a phone conversation exceeds thirty minutes (way beyond our attention span), we get antsy and distracted.

We have been criticized by previous generations for this texting phenomenon. We have been told we don't know how to communicate anymore. For the record, that is total BS*! Texting does not take away our ability to communicate —it just gives us a chance to breathe while we do so and takes the pressure off having to return a call or focus our full attention on a conversation that's not very important. We don't need to call someone to find out what they're doing tonight, a quick text will do the trick.

We've also been the ass of the joke because we now consider a phone call to be romantic when it comes to relationships. Well… it sort of is!

You may think that's stupid, but in reality, to us Millennials, it means the person is taking their valuable time to call, to hear our voice, and as long as we feel the same about the person, this is a romantic gesture! Call it what you like, but we call it *love*. Proving there is still a time when a call over-rules a text, but only in certain situations.

Technology is our best and worst friend. It has caused so much convenience, but with so much pain and grief. Who could foresee relationships ending over invading other people's email accounts and going through their text messages? Girls selling their bodies over the Internet? Something like the *Craigslist killer* even existing?

Nevertheless, this same technology has granted us so many opportunities to stay in touch. Soldiers can now FaceTime or Skype often with their families back home (which I totally wish would have existed when my Dad was deployed). Friends across the globe can feel involved in each other's lives in a matter of seconds. I get to see my nephew's precious little face at the touch of a button; he knows who his aunt is purely because of this.

When you stand back and take a look at technology as a whole, it's scary, but realizing you only have control over your own actions, not what someone else is going to post, write, or comment is key.

You are responsible for your own affairs, and that is what you are limited to. Once I truly understood this, it became more liberating, less frustrating, and easier not to react to the negative shit going on.

In fact, many social figures have hired people to manage their social media accounts so they don't have to deal with this nonsense. While that is sad, it is a factor of being in the limelight and staying relevant. Many of us make the choice to include all kinds of people in our personal life because we showcase our opinions and photos with the rest of the world. So, with that, we must accept the naysayers will come.

I know I only scratched the bare surface of this topic with so many layers and components, but in conclusion we will continue to be technology advancers because that is who we are and frankly that is what we know.

We will have to grow thicker skin and weed through the ruthless comments, but also realize that no one is immune to this – we're in it together.

Flying cars, robots, and cloning? I'm not sure if we're ready, but hey-- bring it on! There's no stopping this.

LULU

# TEN

Allow me…

As we all know, YOLO (You Only Live Once) is a term that is near and dear to the hearts of Millennials. Although it was an amazing excuse for us to party and not give AF*, it's played out. Therefore, it only seems appropriate that I come up with a fresh acronym that upholds the "yolo" standard while incorporating what this book is all about.

LULU: Live Unapologetically, Love Unconditionally.

I want LULU to feel like comfort food to us over-analyzing, anxiety-driven young adults. It's meant to remind us to chill out, be present in the moment, live it up, love one another, all while taking risks.

*Living Unapologetically*

It's about putting your fears aside, biting the bullet and going after what it is you really want in life. It's about putting your dreams in the forefront and your nightmares behind you. It's about being open to hearing what others have to say, but not letting negative projections alter your path. Being unapologetic is making a statement that you're going to live your best life without explanation. It's about not caring what others will think or how you will be judged. It's about letting go of the doubt and doing WTF* you want because it makes you happy.

All of us have experienced a point in time where we felt the opposite. A time where it felt like the roof caved in, the rug was ripped out from under us— moments we were not expecting and were extremely difficult to comprehend. Moments we've felt betrayed or let down, but we had to get back up and keep on going.

Through these experiences we've come to learn that nothing is permanent; not a feeling, not a material item, not any person, but in fact *all* of this is temporary, every last bit of it. Life is going to let us down time and time again. Ultimately, there's nothing we can do about that. However, we can change how we live and view situations. We can stop beating ourselves up over petty BS*.

Time is the most precious gift we are given; so, what better way to live this life than *unapologetically*.

We are here on earth for such a short and unpredictable amount of time, so why waste any of it worrying or being unhappy? Now, before you crucify me for my Millennial, carefree, nonchalant attitude, allow me to explain…

Growing up a lot of Millennials heard, don't do **x** or **y** will happen.

*"Don't drive there or your car will be stolen."*

*"Don't go out tonight or you will fail your test tomorrow and never get into college."*

What I came to realize was that our parents and mentors were trying to be realistic and save us from all the hurt in the world. They want us to understand that sometimes failure can be a blessing in disguise, a chance to reinvent yourself per say. While I can appreciate that, I don't think you necessarily need to fail to learn life lessons.

However, as a young adult I had to break this thought pattern, because this type of fear just doesn't fit with my lifestyle. I can't worry on a daily basis how my future is going to turn out and how every decision I make or every risk I take is affecting the next. Nah, I would be taking Xanax every damn day!

Had I not been able to escape this thought pattern or my comfort zone, I would never have lived in NYC or LA. I would not have traveled to over 20 different countries. I most certainly wouldn't be pursuing my dreams.

I would be working a nine-to-five desk job that didn't satisfy me, and I'd probably be settled down by now with someone I wasn't too crazy about with a kid or two living in a small rural town—blah blah blah. Such a scary thought for me!

However, I broke the cycle and I was able to take the good from what I was taught. In fact, I think it had a lot of positive influence on the way I am now. I am very appreciative for that.

What LULU means to me is being unapologetic, but calculated in my risk-taking. I look at my risks as advancements in my life.

Moving back to Los Angeles from New York City

with no secure job was a *huge* risk for me and a lot of older adults in my life asked me to reconsider. Sorry not sorry. I knew it was something I had to do for myself.

I made sure I had enough money saved to take care of myself for at least 9 months (worst case scenario), and more importantly, I had a plan. I didn't leave NYC with my arms thrown in the air thinking, *"I don't know what I'm going to do when I get there, but LA, here I come!"*

No. I had a plan in mind. Did everything play out exactly as planned? Of course not, but I knew what I had to do to make the move beneficial. A dreamer without a plan of action will always just be a dreamer. Taking that risk and putting any dream to action is what turns it into a reality and most likely into a success.

I look back on the mistakes I've made and I'm unapologetic because I learned from them. I realized that there are more effective ways to handle issues and prepare besides regretting the past and worrying about the future. Stop over-planning; most plans get messed up anyway. Over-planning is assuming you know every variable, and you rarely ever do. So instead of planning every detailed step in life (ones you have no control over), and worrying what is going to happen next, Live Unapologetically!

*Love Unconditionally*

This one is pretty self-explanatory, but I know that many Millennials, along with every other generation, could always use the reminder. You can't live a completely fulfilled life unless you learn to let go; let go of grudges, of hate, of all the mess that's holding you back. Loving unconditionally, is not limited to romantic love, I'm talking about *agape* -- love for everyone around you. It is obviously not easy by any means. It's a lot of work to master, but once you start taking the right steps, it will make your life feel effortless. When we stop competing and start helping one another, this world will be a different place. Grasping the concepts of "pay it forward" and "there's enough wealth to go around" will transform all our lives tremendously.

When we respond to situations with no other emotion than love, our relationships will flourish. Trust me, I have not mastered this concept by any means. However, just practicing the idea and keeping it in the back of my thoughts helps me immensely. We are all facing different trials and tribulations, I can't say it enough: *we are all in this together*. If we could figure this out we would all succeed.

Overall, LULU stands for opening yourself up to all possibilities and giving yourself a chance at the life you know you deserve, while being a good person along the way. It is a very powerful vibration.

**LULU is the opposite mindset of living in fear!**
Live Unapologetically, Love Unconditionally.

So, here's the no-brainer: One shot at this life here on Earth in this body is all we get, so spend less time worrying about the future and more time enjoying the present with your friends, family, and the people around you. Do more activities you enjoy, take that vacation you want, make memories, laugh, enjoy, and let go of all the fears of future obstacles that forbid you to act as if today is all that is guaranteed.

*Staying in your comfort zone and never achieving your dreams should be your worst nightmare.*

So, live your best life!
Also, make up your own acronym and apply it accordingly because, well…why the hell not?

# WHAT'S *NEXT*?

# ELEVEN

About three years ago, a very good friend from college told me that motivational speaking should be a professional path I take in life. I was extremely blown away by this statement. I thought, wait a minute. Do you know me? I mean sure, I give decent advice I guess, but how am I going to help others? I feel a thousand different emotions every single day, I still find myself to be so lost from time to time and, frankly, I'm not sure I have any of this figured out.

Who would want to listen to me? What do I have to offer? What she said next I will never forget because it changed my thought pattern about myself forever. It instilled the confidence in me I had been lacking.

She said to me (via text), and I quote:

*"You have a realistic grasp on life through the things you continue to do and the measures you set for yourself;*

*as well as your reflective nature which ultimately dictates change. You possess qualities that I feel can transform the minds of individuals who are still searching for their own journey and struggle with being oppressed by the fears projected on them by their families, peers, or even themselves while they seek to achieve their own goals."*

The fact that she saw all of this in me completely blew my mind. It made me realize that I don't always have to have the absolute "right" answers for others or myself in order to be helpful. For all of us, it's all about reflection, and that reflection ultimately dictating change, as she put so eloquently.

Then it really clicked for me. I don't need all the answers; in fact, I don't *want* them! I don't want to know if every decision I've made has been right or wrong. I don't want to know where I'm going to be in five years. Instead, I choose to stay present and let the future work itself out because time flies and we'll get there soon enough. I don't want any perceptions of what it *should* look like, to interfere with me being so grateful for what it *is*.

Seriously what are these expectations we give ourselves? Why do we put so much pressure on ourselves? Why do we stress ourselves out so much? WHY?

Ultimately, we Millennials don't know where this journey is going to take us and really that's the fun in it all! Not knowing how each day is going to influence the next. How each decision plays a role in the next chapter of your life.

We are mid-rollercoaster because we're not done making our mark. So, as this may be the conclusion of my book, it's only *the beginning* of a new expedition for you!

With that being said, there are three Millennial

mindsets I want you to think about and take with you on your journey.

First: **Figure out who you are**

Not your race, ethnicity, skin color or hair color, but internally—*who are you?* What type of person are you or do you want to be? If we were all forced to walk around fully covered from head to toe with no form of expressing ourselves other than our actions and our words, how would people know you? What would make them remember you or even interest them in getting to know you? What are your morals and values? What are your convictions? What makes you tic? Really do the core work and get to know yourself on the inside.

We are all given our own talents and gifts, so use them. It is your sole responsibility to make the most of your life. You are the one held accountable.

Finding yourself is a process, and it takes a lot of internal work, but I promise you, it's the best investment you'll ever make. Discover your worth and what good you can bring to yourself and more importantly to the world around you.

Second: **Choose happiness.**

It is your innate right to be happy.

The state of being happy is an emotion, and we can pick our emotions. Emotions are how we react to the situations we are put in, but ask yourself—who picks your reactions? Who chooses if you lose your temper when you are mad, smile when you are happy, or cry when you are sad? Obviously you do.

Many years ago, someone told me "you as an adult have as much control over these emotions as you do over how you dress yourself in the morning". It has always stuck with me because it is one hundred percent true. If you are capable of picking out what to wear then you most certainly are capable of choosing how to act or react. It's the analogy for being in control.

Therefore, it can be said that you can choose to be happy in any situation. Granted, it is definitely not always an easy choice, and it takes a hell of a lot of self-control and self-awareness, but it is possible.

You can wake up each and every morning and smile; automatically emitting the emotion of happiness. You can train yourself to think like this and to be happy. You can write a list that covers everything you are grateful for and recite it over and over. Whatever works for you.

Knowing you have this ability, why would you choose anything else? If you're not happy and feel trapped, then stop bitching about it and change your situation so you can be happy. It's that simple. Stop making excuses for yourself not to be happy.

Third: **Respond with love.**

Building off of LULU, this is the most important one to remember and the most difficult one to maintain. Sometimes we don't always feel like loving others or ourselves, but it is the reason we are all here. It's the reason humans aren't just ants working on a hill. It's the reason we aren't robots and are able to express ourselves.

Our emotions are what differentiate us, and love is the strongest of our emotions. It has more health benefits than you can imagine.

People will be drawn to you, and inevitably, things will start going your way, because the universe has no choice but to be submissive and give back to you what you are exuding. Love is what we're all looking for. Unconditional love: agape love.

There you have it my friends; the Unapologetic: a generation that can't even… in a nutshell. Our generation is so powerful and we're currently in full swing. I can't wait to see all the other incredible advancements we will make in the world.

Go chase your dreams, go conquer the world! Continue to ride the rollercoaster - being one hundred percent UNAPOLOGETIC!

# WORKS CITED

1 --- (2015). *Angel Card Reading Information*. Retrieved December 18, 2015 from, http://www.angelcardreading.org/angel-numbers-911/

2 --- (2015). *911 Angel Numbers*. Brick, NJ: SOULutions, LLC. Retrieved December 18, 2015 from, http://www.spiritualitysolutions.com/911

3 --- Wilson, M. & Gerber, L.E. (2008). *How Generational Theory Can Improve Teaching: Strategies for Working with the "Millennials"*. In Teaching and Learning, Volume 1(1), Fall 2008, pg 29-44.

4 --- The Council of Economic Advisers. (2014). *15 Economic Facts about Millennials*. Executive Office of the President of the United States. October 2014.

5 --- Parramore, L.S. (2014). *Surprise: A Majority of Millennials Don't Have a College Degree—That's Going to Cost Everybody*. AlterNet. Retrieved December 18, 2015 from, http://www.alternet.org/education/surprise-majority-Millennials-dont-have-college-degree-thats-going-cost-everybody

6 --- Grasz, J. (2013). *One-Third of College-Educated Workers Do Not Work in Occupations Related to their College Major*. Chicago: CareerBuilder. Retrieved December 18, 2015 from, http://www.careerbuilder.com/share/aboutus/pressreleasesdetail.aspx?sd=11%2f14%2f2013&siteid=cbpr&sc_cmp1=cb_pr790_&id=pr790&ed=12%2f31%2f2013

7 --- Carnevale, A.P., Smith, N., Strohl, J. (2010). *Projections of Jobs and Education Requirements through 2018*. Georgetown University Center for Education and the Workforce: Help Wanted, June 2010.

8 ---- Westhues, K. (2007). *Mobbing and the Virginia Tech Massacre*. University of Waterloo. Retrieved December 18, 2015 from, http://www.kwesthues.com/vtmassacre.htm

9 ---- Masci, D. (2016). *Q&A: Why Millennials are less religious than older Americans*. Washington, D.C.: Pew Research Center. Retrieved February 1, 2016 from, http://www.pewresearch.org/fact-tank/2016/01/08/qa-why-Millennials-are-less-religious-than-older-americans/

10 ---- Carrey, J. (2014). *Jim Carrey Commencement speech: Full Video & Transcript*. Fairfield, Iowa: Maharishi University of Management. Retrieved February 21, 2016 from, **https://www.mum.edu/whats-happening/graduation-2014/full-jim-carrey-address-video-and-transcript/**

# THIS
# MILLENNIAL

Born a world traveler, raised in a military family, Traci Propst is a writer, Certified Life Coach, and on-air personality.

She is an advocate for her Millennials and strives to give everyone a more positive understanding on the generation as a whole.

She is a young innovator of social change and has hosted many programs geared towards educating peers and encouraging others to take a stand.

She intends on continuing to use her strong voice and platform to portray her perspective and bring a more positive note to all current affairs.

FOLLOW TRACI FOR THE LATEST UPDATES

Tracipropst.com

FB: @TraciPropst
IG: @TraciPropst
TW: @TraciPropst

Made in the USA
Las Vegas, NV
20 August 2021

28539457R00066